Additional Praise for
The Little Book of Safe Money

"There are two parts to investing. One part seeks gains. The other part—too often overlooked—protects your standard of living when markets go bad. Jason Zweig brilliantly focuses on 'protection,' not only in bond investing but in stocks, as well. He names, and knocks, the products designed to part you from your money, while steering you toward the kinds of low-cost, low-risk investments that, historically, have come out ahead."

—Jane Bryant Quinn, financial columnist and author of *Smart and Simple Financial Strategies for Busy People*

"I've been a financial planner for over 30 years and there is not one client I've worked with who would not profit from reading and heeding the advice in *The Little Book of Safe Money*."

—Harold Evensky, President, Evensky & Katz

THE LITTLE BOOK
OF
SAFE MONEY

Little Book Big Profits Series

In the *Little Book Big Profits* series, the brightest icons in the financial world write on topics that range from tried-and-true investment strategies to tomorrow's new trends. Each book offers a unique perspective on investing, allowing the reader to pick and choose from the very best in investment advice today.

Books in the *Little Book Big Profits* series include:

The Little Book That Beats the Market, in which Joel Greenblatt, founder and managing partner at Gotham Capital, reveals a "magic formula" that is easy to use and makes buying good companies at bargain prices automatic, enabling you to successfully beat the market and professional managers by a wide margin.

The Little Book of Value Investing, in which Christopher Browne, managing director of Tweedy, Browne Company, LLC, the oldest value investing firm on Wall Street, simply and succinctly explains how value investing, one of the most effective investment strategies ever created, works, and shows you how it can be applied globally.

The Little Book of Common Sense Investing, in which Vanguard Group founder John C. Bogle shares his own time-tested philosophies, lessons, and personal anecdotes to explain why outperforming the market is an investor illusion, and how the simplest of investment strategies—indexing—can deliver the greatest return to the greatest number of investors.

The Little Book That Makes You Rich, in which Louis Navellier, financial analyst and editor of investment newsletters since 1980, offers readers a fundamental understanding of how to get rich using the best in growth-investing strategies. Filled with in-depth insights and practical advice, *The Little Book That Makes You Rich* outlines an effective approach to building true wealth in today's markets.

The Little Book That Builds Wealth, in which Pat Dorsey, director of stock analysis for leading independent investment research provider Morningstar, Inc., guides the reader in understanding "economic moats," learning how to measure them against one another, and selecting the best companies for the very best returns.

The Little Book That Saves Your Assets, in which David M. Darst, a managing director of Morgan Stanley, who chairs the firm's Global Wealth Management Asset Allocation and Investment Policy Committee, explains the role of asset allocation in maximizing investment returns to meet life objectives. Brimming with the wisdom gained from years of practical experience, this book is a vital road map to a secure financial future.

The Little Book of Bull Moves in Bear Markets, in which Peter D. Schiff, president of Euro Pacific Capital, Inc., looks at historical downturns in the financial markets to analyze what investment strategies succeeded and shows how to implement various bull moves so that readers can preserve, and even enhance, their wealth within a prosperous or an ailing economy.

The Little Book of Main Street Money, in which Jonathan Clements, award-winning columnist for the *Wall Street Journal* and a director of the new personal finance service myFi, offers 21 commonsense truths about investing to help readers take control of their financial futures.

The Little Book of Safe Money, in which Jason Zweig, best-selling author and columnist for the *Wall Street Journal*, shows the potential pitfalls all investors face and reveals not only how to survive but how to prosper in a volatile and unpredictable economy.

THE LITTLE BOOK

OF
SAFE MONEY

How to Conquer Killer Markets,
Con Artists, and Yourself

JASON ZWEIG

WILEY
John Wiley & Sons, Inc.

Published by John Wiley & Sons, Inc., Hoboken, New Jersey.
Published simultaneously in Canada.

For general information on our other products and services or for technical support, please contact our Customer Care Department within the United States at (800) 762-2974, outside the United States at (317) 572-3993 or fax (317) 572-4002.

Wiley also publishes its books in a variety of electronic formats. Some content that appears in print may not be available in electronic books. For more information about Wiley products, visit our web site at www.wiley.com.

Library of Congress Cataloging-in-Publication Data:

Zweig, Jason.
    The little book of safe money : how to conquer killer markets, con artists, and yourself / Jason Zweig.
      p.   cm. — (Little book big profits series)
    ISBN 978-0-470-39852-4 (cloth)
     1. Investments. 2. Portfolio management. I. Title.
  HG4521.Z94 2010
  332.6—dc22

                                                   2009035148

Printed in the United States of America

10 9 8 7 6 5 4 3 2 1

For Mark Cornell and Eric Schmuckler

Shaped by the wise
Who gazed in breathing wonderment,
And left us their brave eyes
To light the ways they went.

Contents

Foreword   xv

Introduction   xxi

Chapter One
The Three Commandments   1

Chapter Two
Solid, Liquid, or Gas?   5

Chapter Three
You Are an Egg   19

Chapter Four
Keeping Your Cash from Turning into Trash   31

Chapter Five
Guarantees Are Not All They're
     Cracked Up to Be   45

Chapter Six
Fixing Your Fixed Income   53

Chapter Seven
Stocks for the Wrong Run   67

Chapter Eight
Rules for Stock Investors to Live By   77

Chapter Nine
Little Things Mean a Lot   89

Chapter Ten
How to Get Your Kids through
     College without Going Broke   99

Chapter Eleven
What Makes Ultra ETFs Mega-Dangerous   107

Chapter Twelve
Hedge Fund Hooey 117

Chapter Thirteen
Commodity Claptrap 131

Chapter Fourteen
Spicy Food Does Not Equal Hot Returns 141

Chapter Fifteen
**WACronyms: Why Initials Are So
    Often the Beginning of the End** 149

Chapter Sixteen
Sex 157

Chapter Seventeen
Mind Control 167

Chapter Eighteen
Financial Planning Fakery 183

Chapter Nineteen
Advice on Advice   189

Chapter Twenty
Fraudian Psychology   199

Chapter Twenty-One
The Terrible Tale of the Missing $10 Trillion   211

Chapter Twenty-Two
How to Talk Back to Market Baloney   219

Acknowledgments   229

Foreword

⁓

Jason Zweig, simply put, is the reigning gold medalist in the investing Olympics decathlon.

Allow me to explain. Investing success does not accrue to those with savant-like expertise in one field of intellectual endeavor, but rather rests on four pillars: a command of financial theory, a working knowledge of financial history, an awareness of financial psychology, and a solid understanding of how the financial industry operates. Like the decathlon winner, the successful investor is rarely the world champion in a single event, but rather someone who excels at *all*.

Few can match Jason's grasp of investment theory, and I am hard-pressed to name anyone who exceeds his knowledge of investment history or the cognitive neuropsychological aspects of finance. Extol the virtues of Ben Graham's magisterial *Security Analysis*, and Jason will ask which edition you're referring to. Mention to him the gambling proclivities of medicated Parkinson's disease sufferers, and then this neurologist soon finds himself humbled by an informed précis of the latest paper on the topic from *Archives of Neurology*.

Finally, over a professional lifetime as a beat reporter at *Forbes*, *Money*, and the *Wall Street Journal*, Jason has gotten to know the industry as well as anyone: who's been naughty, who's been nice, and who will soon be getting unwanted judicial attention in the Southern District of Manhattan. His output in this area has been so prodigious that he hasn't had the time to submit much of his best work for publication. Few investment professionals, for example, are unaware of his classification scheme that cleaves the mutual fund world into a tiny minority of *investment* companies, which focus exclusively on their fiduciary responsibility to their customers, and the overwhelming mass of *marketing* companies, concerned only with their bottom lines. Although Jason has of late made this piece available on his web site,* you will not find it immortalized anywhere between hard or soft covers.

*www.jasonzweig.com/wip/documents/speeches/Serving2Masters.doc

Jason thus has a great deal to offer all investors, from the rankest amateur to the most grizzled pro. Let's sample just a few of his pearls from each of the four events in the investing Olympics:

- *The theory of investing.* Diversification and liquidity are dandy, but they both vanish when we need them the most. As 2008 began, millions of investors owned short-term bond funds holding securities ranging in safety from plain-vanilla high-grade corporate debt to more exotic asset-backed vehicles; a small but soon-to-be-highly-visible minority of funds actually juiced their returns by writing credit default swaps. In normal times, these securities were highly liquid, that is, easily exchangeable for cold, hard cash. When push came to shove in the fall of that year, however, shareholders in need of cash suddenly found that they were worth less than they ever thought possible—in some cases, a lot less. Similarly, during the great bull market of 2002–2007, investors piled into mutual funds specializing in emerging markets and real estate investment trusts (REITs)— ostensibly because of their diversification value, but in reality because their recent performance had been red-hot. In the ensuing market collapse, the diversification value of these two asset classes disappeared faster than taco chips at a Super Bowl party, falling, in some cases, 60 to 70 percent. (In truth, REITs and emerging markets stocks *do* offer substantial diversification benefit, but only if held for the long term: during the 10-year period from 1999 to 2008, these two asset classes provided investors with salutary returns, while the S&P 500 lost money.)

- *The history of investing.* The stock market is not as agreeable a place as many would have you believe. Forget the "stocks for the long run" bias inherent in both the pre- and post-1926 databases used by almost all academics and practitioners. Jason demolishes this paradigm with an efficiency rarely seen this side of a Chuck Norris film: Stock markets do *not* become less risky with time, do *not* always return more than bonds, and *do* vanish, with alarming regularity, into the mists of history.

- *The psychology of investing.* Your own worst enemy is the image in the mirror; this goes double if you're a guy. As I read Jason's sections on the investing heart of darkness inside all of us, I trembled that they might fall into the wrong hands: a snappy ticker symbol, for example, is worth a several-percent stock price premium. Of course, when it comes to manic-depressive behavior, few can hold a candle to Mr. Market himself, and the sooner you stop becoming his anxious codependent and learn to administer to him the tough love he deserves, the wealthier you will be.

- *The business of investing.* Beware of geeks bearing gifts: Most financial innovation serves roughly the same purpose as the pickpocket's decoy, the innocent-appearing chap who bumps into you or asks you the time while his deft accomplice relieves you of your wallet. In much the same way, over the past decade hedge funds, bond funds with clever options strategies, and structured investment vehicles have considerably lightened investor's wallets.

To paraphrase Rabbi Hillel, enough commentary from me. Turn the page and begin to explore investing's essential truths with one of its best tour guides.

—WILLIAM J. BERNSTEIN

Introduction

⁓

After the two bullish decades of the 1980s and 1990s, in the new millennium there has been nowhere for investors to run and nowhere to hide. Just about everything and everyone has lost money in the worst—and most globally interconnected—financial crisis since the Great Depression.

Keeping your money safe has gone from being a luxury to being an absolute necessity. Investors can no longer count on rising markets and trusted relationships to bail out their portfolios for them.

How bad have the past few years been?

At 4 P.M. on November 20, 2008, when the closing bell finally clanged out the end of another disastrous day's trading on the New York Stock Exchange, the bellwether Standard & Poor's 500-stock index (S&P 500) was down 48.8 percent since the beginning of the year. That was not merely the worst performance for the U.S. stock market since its 43.3 percent annual loss in 1931; had 2008 ended that day, the year would have ranked 194th out of the 194 years since 1815.

From the U.S. stock market peak on October 9, 2007, to its trough on March 9, 2009, investors lost $11.2 trillion. Another $14.7 trillion went up in smoke elsewhere around the globe. In 17 murderous months, 60 percent of the world's stock market wealth was destroyed.*

Even after a bounce back in 2009, we have already endured one of the most terrible setbacks for the financial markets in history—and investors' nerves remain shattered, much the way the survivors of an aerial bombardment flinch whenever airplanes whistle overhead. The holders of stocks, bonds, real estate, commodities, mutual funds, hedge funds, even supposedly ultrasafe cash accounts, have been ravaged by losses they never expected and never protected themselves against.

It is not just those at the bottom of the investing totem pole who have suffered. The world's largest insurance company, American International Group (AIG), went bust

*Source: Dow Jones Market Data Group.

buying securities so complex its own managers were incapable of understanding them. Billionaires, hedge-fund moguls, and Swiss bankers lost their shirts in the $13 billion Ponzi scheme run by the smooth-talking Bernie Madoff, former chairman of the NASDAQ stock market. Investment bankers, financial advisers, and risk analysts at firms like Lehman Brothers, Merrill Lynch, and Morgan Stanley were devastated when the company stock they had loaded up on in their retirement plans was wiped out. Professional investors in the mortgage-securities market lost roughly $1.5 trillion after expert analysts at credit-rating agencies like Moody's Investors Service and Standard & Poor's gave the official blessing to investments that turned out to be little better than financial sewage. Many securities with the pristine AAA rating lost more than half their value in a matter of months.

In fact, it has gotten to the point where using the word *security* as a synonym for *investment* does not just seem quaint or old-fashioned; it seems absurd.

Not very long ago, you might have felt confident that wealth and comfort were within your reach, that you could trade up to the house of your dreams, that you could put all your kids through college, and that your retirement would be golden. Now you worry whether you will even be able to make ends meet from day to day.

The Little Book of Safe Money is a survival guide for the most frightening times investors have faced in at least three-quarters of a century. How can you salvage what is left of your money and shelter it from further damage? Can you make it grow without compromising safety? Whom should you trust for advice? How will you ever find the heart to invest again?

Like dieting, investing is simple but not easy. There are only two keys to losing weight: eat less, exercise more. Nothing could be simpler. But eating less and exercising more are not easy in a world full of chocolate cake and Cheetos, because temptation is everywhere. The keys to investing are just as simple: diversify, keep costs low, buy and hold. But those simple steps are not easy for investors bombarded by get-rich-quick e-mail spam, warnings to get out of (or into) the market before it's too late, and television pundits who shriek out trading tips as if their underpants were on fire. Thus *The Little Book of Safe Money* is not only about what you should do, but also about what you must *not* do, in order to build your wealth and safeguard your future. After each chapter you will find "Safe Bets," a series of do's and don'ts that should help make investing not only simpler but also easier.

Let's get started.

Chapter One

The Three Commandments

*What You Should Inscribe
Upon the Stone Tablets
of Your Portfolio*

THERE ARE THREE CENTRAL RULES for keeping your money safe. We will come back to them again and again throughout this book. I call these rules the Three Commandments; they are simple but universal enough to cover virtually every challenge you will face in managing your money.

(That's why there are only three, instead of ten.) If you obey them, you will have a purer investing heart—and better results—than many professional investment managers, who stray constantly from the true path of righteous safety.

I will express the Three Commandments in Biblical language, because they are that important.

All the rest is commentary.

The First Commandment

—————————— ∾ ——————————

Thou shalt take no risk that thou needst not take.

—————————————————————

Always ask yourself: Is this risk necessary? Are there safer alternatives that can accomplish the same objective? Have I studied the pros and cons of each before settling on this choice as the single best way to achieve my goal?

Unless you ask, do not invest.

The Second Commandment

—————————— ∾ ——————————

Thou shalt take no risk that is not most certain to
reward thee for taking it.

—————————————————————

Always ask yourself: How do I know this risk will be rewarded?

"Most certain to reward thee" does not mean that there is zero chance that you will not be rewarded. It does mean, and must mean, that you are *highly likely* to be rewarded. What is the historical evidence, based on the real experience of other investors, to suggest that this approach will actually succeed? During the periods in the past when it hasn't worked—and every investment in history has gone through such dry spells, regardless of what the hypesters might tell you—how big were the losses?

Unless you ask, do not invest.

The Third Commandment

Thou shalt put no money at risk that thou canst not afford to lose.

Always ask yourself: Can I stand to lose 100 percent of this money? Have I analyzed not merely how much I will gain if I am right, but how much I can lose and how I will overcome those losses if I turn out to be wrong? Will my other assets and income be sufficient to sustain me if this investment wipes me out? If I lose every penny I put into this idea, can I recover from the damage?

Unless you ask, do not invest.

Safe Bets

- Never invest without thinking twice and consulting the Three Commandments.

- Answer the questions that accompany the Three Commandments above whenever you invest; they will help you shape an *investment policy*, telling you not only where to put your money but why.

Chapter Two

Solid, Liquid, or Gas?

*Taking to Heart the
Central Lesson of the
Financial Crisis*

THE IDEAL PORTFOLIO is solid and liquid at the same time. Perhaps because this principle defies our normal notions of physics, it's easy for investors to overlook it.

An investment is solid if decades of historical evidence indicate that it is highly unlikely ever to lose the vast majority of its market value.

An investment is liquid if you can transform it into pure cash any time you want without losing more than a few drops. If you can't, then we say that its liquidity has frozen, dried up, or vaporized.

Some investments are solid without being liquid. Unless you borrowed far too much against it, your house is probably worth several hundred thousand dollars even after the recent plunge in real-estate prices—but good luck if you need to convert it to cash in a hurry. There's nothing inherently wrong with having some of your money in illiquid assets; they often have higher returns in the long run. But it is absolutely mandatory for you to keep a reservoir of liquidity in your portfolio at all times. Just as travelers in the wilderness die without water, investors perish if they have no liquidity.

The flip side, of course, is that many investments can appear to be liquid without actually being solid. And they will stay liquid only for as long as everyone continues to pretend that they're solid. These assets offer merely the illusion of liquidity. The mortgage-backed securities created in the credit binge of the past decade were a form of this illusion. In 2006 and 2007, they traded in immense volumes. That made them seem liquid. But the assets underlying these securities—underresearched loans on overpriced homes that were overleveraged by underqualified owners—were not solid at all. So the liquidity was not sustainable.

It was an illusion, like a mirage of water rippling over a patch of sand in a desert.

Just as it would never occur to you, as you step to the kitchen sink to fill up your water glass, that nothing might come out when you turn the faucet, investors never imagine that a previously liquid investment will suddenly turn out to be illiquid. But it can, and it was this shocking discovery, more than anything else, that accounted for the panic among investors in 2008.

The biggest risk of all to your money is the risk that many investors never think about until it is too late: namely, the chance that if you need to turn an asset into cold, hard cash right away, you might not be able to do it. This chapter will help you understand safety in a new way and build a portfolio that should never run dry.

How Leverage Dries Up Liquidity

An investment is liquid if, and only if:

- at least one person is willing to sell it,
- at least one person is willing to buy it,
- *at the same time,*
- for *close to the asking price,*
- the costs of completing the trade are low,
- *and* the buyer and the seller have a secure way to complete the trade.

More often than not, the culprit in a liquidity crisis is leverage, or borrowed money. Miss a few car payments, and the repo man will show up in your driveway with a tow truck. Skip a few mortgage payments, and the bank can lock you out of your house. Borrow to buy stocks that go down in price, and your broker will seize the shares as collateral.

If you *owe*, you do not really *own*.

We all would borrow a lot less if we realized that what *leverage* really means is "giving someone else the right to take my ownership of something away, at the worst possible time for me to lose it." If you lose liquidity in one part of your portfolio, you may suddenly find yourself unable to pay the interest on your debts elsewhere—turning your lenders into the owners of your most coveted assets.

If many people or institutions all leverage up in the same way, the ripple effects can rise into a tidal wave. When Lehman Brothers, the investment bank, collapsed in September 2008, trillions of dollars in complex securities could no longer trade. Billions of dollars in prestigiously rated AAA mortgage bonds could not be priced at all. Leading American companies suddenly found that no one would lend them money even for as little as 24 hours.

And cash itself—the very essence of liquidity—turned out to be frozen. The Reserve Fund, a money-market mutual fund with a sterling reputation, held so much

Lehman Brothers debt that it "broke the buck," informing its investors that their money was no longer worth 100 cents on the dollar and denying them daily access to their accounts.

We tend to think of our most valuable assets as the safest, because their total value is the farthest away from zero. A house worth hundreds of thousands of dollars seems like a safer investment than a bank account with a few hundred dollars in it.

But the central lesson of the recent financial crisis is as plain as the nose on your face: No matter how valuable an investment may be or appear to be, it's of no practical value to you unless it's liquid when you need to cash out. Your house may have been appraised for $1 million in 2006, but if so few people now want it that you might need two or three years to find a buyer at $699,000, then that $1 million is a fantasy. So, for that matter, is $699,000 if you have to wait two or three years to get it.

By definition, no asset can ever be worth more than someone is willing to pay you for it. Without buyers, there is no liquidity; without liquidity, so-called securities have no security.

Can You Tap Liquidity Elsewhere?

Liquidity risk is not hypothetical; it is real. Whenever we invest money now, it is always in the expectation of being able to turn it into even more money later—not money that exists only in our imagination, but actual cash we can spend to fund our future needs. Since life is full of surprises, tomorrow's needs can be swamped by today's emergency. Lose your job, get divorced, fall ill, become disabled, or simply suffer the rising costs of family life—and suddenly you may need to turn your assets into cash not decades down the road, but right now. Then, without a moment's notice, you will lose the luxury of being able to sell your investments at exactly the right time and price. You will, instead, be forced to get rid of them in a fire sale.

Thus, for safety's sake, you must erect the foundation of your financial future not on bedrock but on a reservoir of liquidity. And the only sensible way to do that is by determining the personal liquidity risks in the portfolio you already have. For the simplest starting point, measure your own portfolio against the national average. Exhibit 2.1 shows, in descending order, the percentage of total assets that the average American family holds across 16 categories.

And now we can review, in simplified form, how liquid each of these assets will be—especially when combined with the others. Exhibit 2.2 shows four measures of liquidity for each major asset: how long it may take to sell, how

Exhibit 2.1 The Assets of the Average U.S. Household, 2007

Asset	Percentage of Total Assets*
Home	31.8%
Privately held business	19.6
Retirement accounts	11.7
Other residential property[1]	7.1
Stocks	6.1
Mutual funds[2]	5.4
Cash[3]	3.7
Nonresidential real estate	3.8
Vehicles	2.9
Other managed financial assets[4]	2.2
Bonds	1.4
Certificates of deposit	1.4
Cash-value life insurance	1.1
Other nonfinancial assets[5]	0.9
Other financial assets[6]	0.7
Savings bonds	0.1

Source: Calculations based on "Changes in U.S. Family Finances from 2004 to 2007: Evidence from the Survey of Consumer Finances," www.federalreserve.gov/pubs/bulletin/2009/pdf/scf09.pdf.

Notes:
[1] Second home, time shares, rental properties.
[2] Excluding money-market funds.
[3] Bank accounts and money-market funds.
[4] Annuities, trusts, hedge funds, etc.
[5] Art and collectibles, jewelry, precious metals.
[6] Futures and options, oil and gas leases, royalties, etc.
*Numbers do not sum to exactly 100.0 percent because of rounding.

costly it can be to sell, how much its market value may decline, and how much money people typically borrow against it. The less time it takes you to sell an asset, the lower your expenses in selling it, the less its market price fluctuates, and the less leverage you used to pay for it, the more liquid it is.

How to Keep Liquidity from Evaporating

You can quibble with my assumptions in Exhibit 2.2; in the real world, the numbers may vary widely. But the basic principle is indisputable: You must seek to make your overall portfolio both solid and liquid at the same time. You should not add even more illiquid assets to a portfolio that is illiquid already. Conversely, if your portfolio is already liquid, then you can—and probably should—add some illiquidity in pursuit of higher returns.

Of course, the exact mechanics of how you invest will have a huge impact on your results. If you invest in stocks one company at a time, you could easily rack up expenses of more than 2 percent annually—and, in the end, might lose not just 20 percent to 80 percent of your money, but 100 percent of it. But if you invest in stocks through a low-cost index fund, your expenses will be minuscule and it is highly unlikely that you will lose all your money.

Note, too, that an asset can be more liquid in one dimension than another; for example, you can sell an index

Exhibit 2.2 The Liquidity of the Typical U.S. Household

Asset	Time to Sell	Cost to Sell	Potential Loss from Purchase Price	Leverage	Overall Liquidity	Estimated Market Value *minus* Debt	My Allocation (% of Total)
Home	Several weeks to several years	Up to 6%	10% to 35%	Up to 90%			
Privately held business	Months to years	Up to 10%	25% to 40%	Variable	🚰🚰		
Retirement accounts	0 to 3 days	0% to 5%; tax PEW	20% to 50%	None			
Other residential property	Several weeks to several years	Up to 6%	10% to 35%	Up to 90%			
Stocks	0 to 3 days	1% to 2%	20% to 80% or more	Up to 50%	🚰🚰🚰		
Mutual funds	0 to 3 days	0% to 5%	20% to 50%	Usually none	🚰🚰🚰		
Cash	0 to 3 days	Usually 0%	0% *	None	🚰🚰🚰		
Nonresidential real estate	Several weeks to several years	Up to 6%	10% to 25%	Variable	🚰		
Vehicles	Days to weeks	Up to 20% or more	Varies with age	Up to 100%	🚰		
Other managed financial assets	Often PEW	Up to 7%	20% to 50%	None	🚰🚰🚰		
Bonds	0 to 3 days	1% to 2%	10%	Usually none	🚰🚰		
Certificates of deposit (CDs)	Immediate if at maturity	0% at maturity; PEW	0%	None			
Cash-value life insurance	Variable	Tax PEW	Variable	None			
Other nonfinancial assets	Days to months	10% to 35% or more	50% or more	Usually none	🚰		
Other financial assets	Variable	Variable	Variable	Variable	🚰		
Savings bonds	Immediate if at maturity	0% at maturity; PEW	0%	None	🚰		

Notes: Costs to sell include direct brokerage, agent, or auction fees; trading spreads and discounts to market or appraised value can make total costs considerably higher. Costs to sell small and foreign stocks are higher. Costs to sell U.S. Treasury bonds are below 1%, but less commonly traded bonds can be more costly to sell. PEW—penalty for early withdrawal.

fund investing in U.S. stocks in no time and incur no expenses to unload it, but if the stock market has crashed right before you sell, then you could face a huge loss in market value. If you are foolish enough to hold a leveraged exchange-traded fund (ETF) (see Chapter 11), then your losses not only may be even greater, but are entirely unpredictable.

But, in general, an asset that rates well (or poorly) on one dimension will do so on the others as well. Art and collectibles, for instance, can take a long time to sell, carry heavy transaction costs, trade in fragmentary markets that are prone to fads and fizzles, and may even be subject to borrowing. Collecting Picasso prints, Chippendale chairs, or Beanie Babies can give you a lot of pleasure and pride, but your collection—no matter how valuable—is about as liquid as a bag full of sand.

The purpose of Exhibit 2.2 is very simple: It is a visual tool enabling you to see how exposed you are to the risk of not being able to turn your assets into cash when you need it. Take an evening or a weekend morning to estimate how much each of your assets is worth. You'll need your bank balances, mortgage and car-loan information, brokerage and mutual-fund statements, annuity and insurance contracts, and any other materials to document the approximate value of your assets. You can estimate the current market value of your house at www.zillow.com, www.domania.com, or www.realtor.com, and of your car at www.kbb.com or www.edmunds.com.

Be sure to subtract any loans you owe from the market value of each asset. If your house is worth $500,000 but you have a $400,000 mortgage, then its net value to you is only $100,000.

Once you've made a good-faith effort to add up all your assets and subtract your liabilities, you will have a better sense of how vulnerable your overall wealth is to the risk of illiquidity. Seeing not only each of the pieces, but how they fit together as a whole, will give you a new way of looking at your assets. This template also lets you see how you compare with the average U.S. household. (Hint: The typical American family is dangerously illiquid.)

Let's say your private business is 60 percent of your net worth, and your home equity is 27 percent. Before you even consider upgrading your old jalopy to an expensive new car—which will make you even more illiquid—you should bolster your holdings of cash and bonds.

If, however, most of your wealth is in very liquid assets, you should consider putting new money into investments that are less liquid; you can comfortably withstand a little more risk. (Less liquid assets tend to have the potential for higher returns.) Let's say you suddenly inherit $1 million from Aunt Matilda; there's probably no need for you to keep the entire inheritance in cash. You are now so awash in liquidity that the wise thing to do is to pour some of it off and take some risk with that portion.

As a rule of thumb, you are at risk of a sudden cash drought unless you have enough of your total wealth in highly liquid assets to cover a year's worth of living expenses if you had no other cash coming in. (Don't know how much your annual living expenses come to? You can find an excellent online budgeting tool at The Consumer's Almanac, www.pueblo.gsa.gov/cic_text/money/almanac/calmanac.htm. Other options that can be helpful: www.budgetpulse.com and www.money.strands.com.)

If you don't have a year's worth of liquidity, then you can't just pretend the problem doesn't exist. You have no choice but to spend less and save more until there's enough liquidity in your reservoir to outlast 12 months of drought.

Most professional investors never give their portfolios the kind of simple test of liquidity I'm suggesting for you here. And more of them should have: By late 2008, giant institutions like Harvard University's $37 billion endowment found themselves in such a liquidity bind that they had to sell some assets into a distressed market or even borrow money.

So don't make the same stupid mistake that the so-called smart money made. Take the time to check your own liquidity.

In the ultimate investing paradox, your portfolio cannot be solid unless it is also liquid. In fact, that's the only way to keep your wealth from evaporating!

Safe Bets

- Always look at what you own and what you owe as part of the bigger picture of your total net worth.
- Invest the time it takes to calculate and track your family budget.

Chapter Three

You Are an Egg

~

What's Missing from the Usual Advice about Diversification

THE BIGGEST SINGLE HOLDING in your portfolio is you: the income that your career will generate over the rest of your life. Economists call this your "human capital," and it is at least as important as your financial capital like stocks, bonds, cash, and mutual funds.

So, when you follow the classic and indisputably good advice not to put all your eggs in one basket, remember that you are one of the eggs. You must do everything in your power to ensure that your financial capital and your human capital do not get cracked or scrambled at the same time.

Why? There are several reasons.

If you work at a company that turns out to be the next Enron or Lehman Brothers, then you will end up losing your job, and you may be damaged goods in the eyes of most other employers, at least for a while. The value of your human capital has been impaired. And that's exactly when you need the value of your financial capital to be strong, so that it can tide you over until you can get a new job and start rebuilding your human capital. If you don't have job income, you will have to live at least partly off investment income.

If, however, you invested heavily in your own company and your own industry, then the value of your financial capital will fall in lockstep with the value of your human capital—precisely the all-my-eggs-in-one-basket problem you want to avoid. (Remember: Most of the people who worked at Enron, Lehman, and just about every other company that has gone bust all thought—just like you—that their company had a great future. If they were wrong, you might be, too.)

What if your entire profession suffers a setback? If all your other investments are closely tied to your job and your industry, you could end up out of work and out of money at the same time. Furthermore, if you live in a company town, the value of your house could plummet when management cuts thousands of jobs at once; even the quality of your children's schools could suffer. (Ask anyone who lives in Detroit.) And the value of your human capital will take a huge hit at the same time. That's the risk of putting all your eggs in one basket and having the entire basket get smashed at once.

The Risks of Being You

Let's say you earn $50,000 a year—roughly the median income for a U.S. household—and each year you get a raise averaging 3 percent. Over the next 20 years, you will earn a cumulative total of $1,383,824. Of course, taxes will take a big chunk of that, and you will have living expenses all along the way, so you certainly won't get to *keep* $1,383,824. And a dollar you will get in the distant future is less valuable than a dollar you get today, so your cumulative earnings are worth less than that raw total would indicate. But the present value of your future earnings—what all that income down the road is worth now—is somewhere between $500,000 and $800,000.*

*The differences in present value are determined by the interest rate used to discount the future earnings; at 10 percent, the cumulative future earnings have a present value of slightly over $500,000, while at 5 percent their present value is just under $800,000.

If you earn more than $50,000 now, your future earnings will be much greater.

That should give you some idea of what your most valuable asset really is: It's you. Chances are, you are worth more than your home, your retirement account, or your stock and mutual-fund portfolio. If you are young, you may well be worth far more than all those other assets combined.

But, just like any other asset, you are risky. In order to produce that nearly $1.4 million in cumulative earnings, you need to protect yourself from the risks that human capital is heir to. You must safeguard yourself.*

Your human capital is vulnerable to two kinds of risks: general and specific. General risks threaten everyone's human capital, no matter who you are. Specific risks jeopardize human capital in ways that are unique to your own situation.

The General Risks

In my view, besides the obvious risks of death and disability, there are three general risks to human capital: location, inflation, and alteration.

---

*Your human capital also faces one risk that's a certainty: death. Fortunately, that problem is easy to solve—not biologically, but financially. Go to www.insure.com and get yourself a low-cost term life-insurance policy; for a few hundred dollars a year, you can assure your heirs of a benefit totaling several hundred thousand dollars after you are gone.

1. *Location risk.* If you live in the United States and work for a U.S.-based company that pays you in dollars, you will be in trouble if the American economy goes into a protracted decline and ends up like Germany or Russia after World War I, Great Britain in the 1970s, or Japan in the 1990s. The same is true anywhere around the world at any time: The value of your skills depends largely on where (and when) you happen to live and the health of the national economy that surrounds you. Just as a bear market tends to drag down the value of nearly all stocks, a struggling economy depresses the value of the human capital of almost everyone who lives in that country.

2. *Inflation risk.* Your human capital will grow over time as you become more skilled, experienced, and knowledgeable in your work. (You can also give your human capital a boost in value by furthering your education with special courses or a graduate degree.) With each passing year, companies will be willing to pay more to have the benefit of your expertise. But, at the same time, inflation can erode the purchasing power of your earnings. If $1 this year will buy only 96 cents' worth of goods next year, then the growth in the value of your human capital may not keep pace with the

rising cost of living. If you cannot earn more than you need to spend next year, you will be unable to save to meet your needs in future years—like retirement.

3. *Alteration risk.* Normally, you should be free to alter how—and how much—you work. You could, for example, put in longer hours, take on a second job, freelance in your spare time, or even turn a hobby into a source of extra income. You could relocate to another city (or country) for better pay. You could go back to school for a graduate degree, or take night classes in a job-related field—which, for a few thousand dollars today, could add hundreds of thousands of dollars to your lifetime earnings. Or you could delay your retirement; working more years will not only raise the total value of your human capital but will increase the amount of your monthly Social Security payment once you do retire. However, not everyone has this kind of flexibility. You, or someone in your family, may have health problems that prevent you from taking on any extra demands on your time and energy. Caring for your children or your parents may make it impractical for you to relocate or to go back to school. Or your spouse may simply be unwilling to move to Bangor or Bangalore. In any of these cases, you

face alteration risk, and it can hamper the growth of your human capital.

The Specific Risks

While virtually everyone faces the same general risks to human capital, the specific risks differ widely. You can get a handle on them by thinking hard about the company you work for. Imagine that it's five years in the future, your company has gone bankrupt, and you have the unenviable task of figuring out what went wrong. Did the company depend on a single customer or a single market for too large a proportion of its sales? Was it financing its operations with borrowed money that became prohibitively expensive when interest rates rose? Was it overly vulnerable to a change in the price for its main raw materials? Did a new technology come along and render the company's products or services obsolete?

If you work for a company whose stock is publicly traded, you can glean some of this information by reading the latest annual report, focusing especially on the financial statements, the management discussion and analysis, and the information about risk factors. Then look back at the reports from earlier years. Identify the worst years the company ever had and seek the common external factors that caused sales and profits to go down. Even if the company is private, you and your colleagues should have a general sense of what could hurt or kill the business. Ask the most experienced people in the firm to tell you what the worst time in its history was and what, in their opinion, caused the setback.

Here are a few hypothetical cases.

- If you work for a manufacturer of plastic bottles, the biggest risk is probably a rise in the price of oil, since petrochemicals are the main raw material that your products are made from.
- If you work for a cable company, you should likely be worried most about interest rates, since your company has probably borrowed a great deal of money and rising rates would make paying off the debt prohibitively expensive.
- If you work for a firm that imports all its products from another country, you are vulnerable to political or economic turmoil there.
- If you work on Wall Street, your biggest worry should be a market crash, which will not only cut your bonus pay but make you a lot less employable for the foreseeable future.

Some people's human capital has very little specific risk. As Benjamin Franklin wrote, "In this world nothing can be said to be certain, except death and taxes." So the human capital of funeral-home directors and IRS agents has almost no risk at all. Tenured educators, career officers in the military, prison administrators, and, perhaps, members of the clergy are others who face relatively low risks to their human capital. Their jobs tend to be secure and fairly immune to the fluctuations of the economy around them.

Most of the rest of us are somewhere in between.

Let's say you are a police officer. You may feel your human capital is secure because you provide an essential service to your community. However, your salary comes from the tax base that funds your city's budget. Does a large proportion of that tax revenue come from a single industry—say, energy or banking or computer technology? If so, then the value of your human capital depends on the health of that industry. When the price of energy collapsed in the 1980s, workers of all kinds suffered in "oil patch" cities like Houston. The bursting of the Internet bubble in 2000 to 2002 hurt people throughout Silicon Valley. And the end of the real-estate boom in cities like Las Vegas, Miami, and Phoenix took a bite out of the earnings of many workers there, regardless of whether their jobs were tied directly to the housing market. If the local economy crashes hard enough, not even a seemingly essential job like a police officer may turn out to be completely safe.

Hedging Yourself

How, then, would you reduce the risks to your human capital? There are several techniques you can use.

First, do not put your financial capital into the same basket as your human capital. In 1999 and early 2000, hundreds of people working in the technology industry e-mailed me to mock the columns I had written warning them not to invest in their company stock or in the tech industry. Many of these people had their jobs, retirement money, bonuses, stock options, the value of their homes, and sometimes even the quality of their children's schools all tied to one single factor: the torrid growth of technology. All of their financial capital *and* their human capital faced the same risk at once, and many of them ended up losing 80 to 90 percent of their wealth.

From 2006 to 2008, I heard the same sentiments from people who worked in the oil industry. As the price of oil soared toward $150 a barrel, they pumped everything they had into the thing they knew best—until nearly every aspect of their wealth depended on the price of oil climbing forever higher.

Around the same time, real-estate agents were not only earning their salaries and commissions from selling houses, but were borrowing money to flip houses for a quick profit—and putting some of the proceeds into shares of real-estate funds.

These people have lost their shirts.

It happens all the time. Doctors put their IRAs into healthcare stocks. Bankers speculate on financial sector funds. Farmers buy shares in agricultural-equipment makers. Mechanics buy the stock of carmakers.

All these investors make the deadly mistake of putting their financial capital into the same basket already occupied by their human capital. There's only room for one egg in there. Pile more eggs in, and the ones on top, as well as the one underneath—*you*—may all end up shattered at once.

If you feel you absolutely must invest in your own company's stock, limit your exposure to no more than 10 percent of your total stock portfolio. Resist the temptation to invest in a sector fund that buys other stocks in the same industry you work in. Remember: Your human capital is already at risk in your industry, and you do *not* need to risk your financial capital there, too. Bear in mind the First Commandment: *Thou shalt take no risk that thou needst not take.*

Then look at Treasury Inflation-Protected Securities (TIPS)—U.S. government bonds whose value rises when inflation heats up. Anyone whose human capital is vulnerable to the escalating cost of living should consider investing heavily in TIPS. (Inflation-protected bonds are also issued by many other governments around the world.)

Next, consider investing in whatever might bash your egg basket. If you work for a plastics manufacturer, then you might put a small portion of your money into energy stocks. That way, if oil prices rise and knock down the value of your human capital, the value of your financial capital will go up; the gain in your energy stocks will partly compensate you for the toll that higher oil prices will take on your job security.

The bottom line is simple: Remember, when you are seeking not to put all your eggs in one basket, that you are the biggest egg of all. Make sure your financial capital will not crack at the same time as your human capital. If you can remember this rule, you will have gone a long way toward keeping your money secure.

Safe Bets

- Don't put your financial and human capital in the same basket.
- Do hold TIPS, which will help fend off inflation.
- Do consider investing in assets that should do well when your industry does badly.

Chapter Four

Keeping Your Cash from Turning into Trash

A Safe Investment Becomes Risky When It Goes Off in Hot Pursuit of Higher Return

IN LATE 2008 AND EARLY 2009, terrified investors stampeded into U.S. Treasury bills. Their buying panic drove Treasury prices so high that many of these investors earned a negative yield on their holdings. That guaranteed loss is the price of the fake safety that investors get when they think with their guts instead of their heads.

There is no such thing as absolute safety. Any investment is safe at the right price, but risky at too high a price. The more you pay, the less safe it becomes. The bills, notes, and bonds issued by the U.S. Treasury have traditionally been regarded as the safest of all securities—but their safety, too, is a function of price. Pay too much for them in the first place and you will turn these safe havens into serious hazards.

Investors who put $100,000 into four-week Treasury bills on December 19, 2008, for instance, faced a certain loss of $10 if they held on until January.* Granted, they didn't have to worry that the issuer would default or go bankrupt. But they paid a peculiar price for that peace of mind—a guaranteed small loss. By pursuing safety at all costs, these investors had made their money *un*safe!

That behavior was not just utterly foolish but entirely unnecessary. It was a flagrant violation of the First Commandment: *Thou shalt take no risk that thou needst not take*. With only a bit of extra effort, investors can raise the return and lower the risk on their cash balances.

Source: www.ustreas.gov/offices/domestic-finance/debt-management/ interest-rate/daily_treas_bill_rates_historical_2008.shtml. The loss does not include transaction costs.

High Yield, Low Risk, Fat Chance

First, think about what cash is. It's money that you can convert on demand—without cost, loss, or delay—into goods and services that you need.

Now think about what cash *isn't*. Any asset whose value is fluctuating or uncertain—and thus may not be freely and promptly convertible into 100 cents on the dollar—is not cash.

Short-term bond funds, often sold as being "safe as cash" or as cash equivalents, are no such thing. In 2008, the Schwab YieldPlus short-term bond fund lost 35.4 percent, the Oppenheimer Limited-Term Government Fund dropped 6.3 percent, and the BlackRock Short Term Bond went down 7.1 percent. Each of these funds held risky mortgage securities as a way to juice its yield. When the financial crisis exploded, these funds imploded.

As sure as the sun rising in the east, Wall Street is forever inventing another newfangled way to promise "higher yield at low risk," "safety with more income," or "returns better than cash with no more risk." Any time anyone tries to sell you any investment on premises like these, put one hand on your wallet and run for your life; you are about to be snookered. In the late 1980s, it was government-plus and option-income funds. In the 1990s, it was short-term world income funds.* In the early 2000s, it was short-term bond funds and auction-rate securities. Tragically, time after time, investors have been told the same fairy tales about low risk and high yield—right before they lost a huge chunk of their hard-earned money.

You can have low risk, or you can have high yield. *But you can never have both in the same investment.* Anyone who tells you otherwise might as well be selling you antigravity pills, music that makes you lose weight while you sleep, or the ability to make a teenager behave by snapping your fingers.

The Money-Market Markdown

That law of financial physics was proved, yet again, in the fall of 2008. A leading money-market fund, which had seemed as exciting as a subcommittee meeting at the Apathy Society of Saskatchewan, detonated in investors' faces.

Money-market funds are required by U.S. regulations to maintain an average overall maturity of 90 days, meaning that most of their return comes from securities with

---

*The mutual-fund industry will not tell you about these failures. Once, there were dozens of funds in these categories, with billions of dollars invested; now, the categories themselves no longer even exist. They have been erased from history, as if they had never been there. But real investors lost hundreds of millions of real dollars in these funds, even though the official industry record ignores those losses.

lives of three months or less. Unlike bonds or bond funds with longer maturities, money-market funds carry virtually no risk of price declines when interest rates change; they simply do not hold on to any securities long enough for that to happen.

Furthermore, in the entire 37-year history of money-market funds, no retail investor in a money-market fund had ever lost a penny. In fact, the $1.00 per share net asset value of money-market funds had come to be taken for granted, a standard benchmark that had essentially never been breached. Deposits in a money-market fund had always been a sure thing: Write a check, call the fund, send a wire, and the cash was yours immediately.

Then came September 15, 2008. Lehman Brothers, the big Wall Street investment bank, had collapsed. The Reserve Primary Fund—the original money-market fund and still one of the biggest, with $63 billion in assets and a sterling reputation—announced without any warning that it had loaded up on securities issued by Lehman. After years of fulminating against the risks of commercial paper (short-term, often unsecured corporate debt), Reserve's co-founder and chairman, Bruce Bent, had plunked half the fund's assets into it.

Because Lehman's bust caught Reserve by surprise, the fund still held $785 million in short-term debt issued by the failed investment bank. There was no market for these securities and no way to evaluate them. With

1.2 percent of its assets in Lehman's debt, Reserve could not assure investors that they would receive 100 cents on the dollar. In fact, on September 16, the fund announced that it was worth only 97 cents per share; many investors would wait weeks, even months, to get their money out. The Reserve Fund had "broken the buck"—failing to honor the universal understanding that its share price would always remain constant at $1.00.*

The results were immediate and drastic. In one of the fastest and starkest panics in modern financial history, investors yanked $123 billion out of money-market funds in the ensuing two weeks.

The situation has since stabilized, and new rules should make money-market funds even safer. But the Reserve fiasco hammered home the importance of the Second Commandment: *Thou shalt take no risk that is not most certain to reward thee for taking it.* And the meltdown also served as a reminder of six basic rules for keeping your cash safe:

1. *A good reputation does not ensure safety.*

   The pioneer in the industry with a pristine record, Reserve still yielded to temptation. Investors must never rely on a manager's past laurels alone.

---

*Steve Stecklow and Diya Gullapalli, "A Money-Fund Manager's Fateful Shift," *Wall Street Journal*, December 8, 2008.

2. *A rapid rise in yield is a red flag.*

At the end of 2004, the average yield of the Reserve Primary Fund Class R over the previous 12 months was 0.39 percent, far below the 0.97 percent yield of the Crane Money Fund Average, showing that Reserve was still sticking to its conservative ways. By the end of August 2008, Reserve—whose yield had been well under half the industry average in 2004—yielded 3.12 percent versus 3.15 percent for the index. The Reserve Fund had lost all reserve. Weeks later, the fund imploded. If your fund's yield (relative to the industry average) ever rises that much this fast, get out.*

3. *Add back the expenses.*

At the end of August 2008, Reserve Primary Fund Class R's yield was almost identical to that of the Crane Money Fund Average—in the standard format, reported after expenses. But Reserve's annual expenses were 1.06 percent, while the expenses of the funds in the index averaged just 0.47 percent. To determine the yield of the underlying securities, add the expenses back in. The fund index held securities with an average yield of

---

*I thank Peter G. Crane, president and publisher, Crane Data LLC, for providing me with the historical data to document this pattern.

3.62 percent (that's the 3.15 percent reported yield of the index, plus 0.47 percent in expenses). The Reserve fund, meanwhile, held securities with an average yield of 4.18 percent (that's the fund's 3.12 percent reported yield, plus its 1.06 percent in expenses). You might not think 4.18 percent is much higher than 3.62 percent, but in the stodgy world of money-market funds, even tiny increases in yield loom large. That fat margin of extra yield—invisible after expenses are deducted— shows that the fund had been gorging on much riskier securities. Thus, one of the simplest tests of a fund's safety is to look at its yield *before* expenses are deducted.

4. *Never pay through the nose.*

Fund managers love to boast that they charge higher fees because they deliver better results, or service, or something. Since every dollar in management fees that you pay to the fund manager will reduce your net yield, the manager must somehow get the yield up if the fund is not to look completely unattractive. The easiest way to do that is to buy securities that pay higher interest because the borrowers are too weak to get credit at lower rates. All else being equal—and it nearly always is—a fund with higher expenses offers lower safety.

Any money-market fund with annual expenses of 0.5 percent or higher is too expensive; in fact, you should be able to find ample choices at 0.25 percent or less. Cheaper is safer.

5. *Watch out for waivers.*

Many fund managers waive—or temporarily skip charging—a portion of their fees in an effort to goose the yield of their funds. According to Morningstar, 63 percent of all money-market funds were waiving at least a portion of their expenses as of 2009. You might not notice unless you get out your microscope. The disclosure comes as footnotes to the table of fees and expenses in a fund's prospectus, in language along these lines: "Ketchum and Steele Fund Management has contractually agreed to waive or reimburse fees or expenses. . . ." Keep reading and you will see that the waiver can usually be eliminated at any time for any reason, leaving you stuck holding a more expensive fund without any warning. To adjust for the fake fees, take the fund's yield for its latest fiscal year. Now subtract the reimbursements, as reported in the table. The resulting figure is the fund's true yield— what it would have earned without the temporary reduction in fees. If you don't like the true yield, don't put money in the fund.

6. *Invest in both tax-exempt and taxable funds.*

It's not a bad idea to have both a tax-free municipal money-market fund and a taxable money-market fund. You can arbitrage, or switch back and forth between them at will, to take advantage of any after-tax difference in their yields. Use the Municipal Bond Tax-Equivalent Yield calculator at www.dinkytown.net (or similar tools elsewhere online, which you can find by Googling "taxable equivalent yield" + "calculator"). Simply enter the fund yield, along with your tax brackets and filing status. The calculator will then show you the after-tax return on each alternative. Taking care to keep the required minimum amount in both funds at all times, you can move most of your money to whichever fund happens to have the higher yield after tax. Often that will be the tax-free fund, but not always—and you should feel free to take advantage of any difference in rates.

In mid-2009, for example, Vanguard's Prime Money Market Fund was yielding 0.52 percent, while its Tax-Exempt Money Market Fund was yielding 0.66 percent. If you input 0.66 percent into the "bond yield" window of the calculator, you will see that you would need to earn 0.88 percent on the taxable Prime fund to retain the same amount after taxes.* Thus the Tax-Exempt fund was, for the time being at least, the better deal.

The Cash Horizon

Now let's put all this together.

Cash is the most basic building block of a portfolio, the cornerstone that holds everything else upright; it also determines how risky everything you erect on top of it will be. A young investor who was 100 percent in stocks (as many reckless financial advisers might have suggested he should be) in October 2007 would have lost 60 percent of his money by March 2009. If he'd kept 20 percent in cash, he would have lost no more than 48 percent; if he'd had 40 percent in cash, his losses would have been no greater than 36 percent. If you keep the cash portion of your portfolio secure, it can hold up the rest of your wealth through the worst of times.

The basic principle of managing your cash sensibly is that you should match the horizon of your assets (the cash) with that of your liabilities (whatever you plan to spend it on). If you will need to spend the money within a year or so, then you should keep it in a government-insured bank

---

*Assumptions: $100,000 in taxable income, 25 percent federal tax bracket, 5 percent state income tax, married filing jointly. Your own figures will vary from these; you can enter the correct numbers in the online calculator. For "bond yield," enter the 30-day yield of the tax-free fund.

deposit or money-market mutual fund. If you will need it one to five years from now, a certificate of deposit could make sense. For spending needs five years or more in the future, Treasury Inflation-Protected Securities (TIPS), which rise in value to keep pace with the rising cost of living, are almost certainly the best bet.

If it's a 401(k) or other retirement account, and you are not yet in your late 50s, then you have decades to go before you will spend any of the money. It makes no sense—zero, nada, zip—for you to keep any portion of a retirement account in a money-market fund. These funds maintain an average overall maturity of 90 days, meaning that most of their return is generated by securities with lives of three months or less. You cannot achieve long-term ends with short-term means; it's foolish to try to fulfill goals that are decades away with portfolios built out of a continuous series of investments that will not last for more than a few weeks at a time.

Instead, long-term investors should keep a sizable portion of their retirement accounts in Treasury Inflation-Protected Securities (or in funds that invest in TIPS). Because TIPS keep pace with inflation, they are close to risk-free, for three reasons:

1. The government stands behind the pledge to repay principal upon maturity, so there is minimal chance of default.

2. The bonds are designed to rise in value as the cost of living goes up, so there is no risk that their purchasing power will be eroded by inflation.

3. If prices fall, in what's called deflation, you are still assured that you will get the full value of your principal back if you hold until maturity.

Since the biggest risk to your future lifestyle is the chance that your savings will not have kept up with rising prices over the intervening decades, TIPS offer an almost perfect insurance policy. Although their short-term prices can be quite volatile, their long-term performance is assured. In real terms—after accounting for inflation—you are highly unlikely to lose money on TIPS (unless the government defaults on its debt, in which case keeping up with rising prices will be the least of your worries). TIPS are the ultimate form of safety: cash with an insurance kicker to cover your future expenses.

Safe Bets

- Do shop for money-market funds by looking for the lowest expenses. Cheaper is better.
- Don't be a sucker for temporary fee reductions that will magically disappear right after you invest.
- Money-market funds don't belong in your retirement account, but TIPS do.

Chapter Five

Guarantees Are Not All They're Cracked Up to Be

~

Every Lock Has a Loophole

W HEN IT COMES TO MINIMIZING the risk that your cash will not be there when you need it, the closest thing to a sure thing is a guarantee that insures you against loss of principal.

Unfortunately, with most guarantees, there's less than meets the eye. The Securities Investor Protection

Corporation (SIPC) was chartered by an act of the U.S. Congress and provides some indemnification against losses when money is stolen or missing from brokerage firms. But that insurance is not provided by the government, nor is it backed by a federal guarantee. SIPC purports to cover up to $500,000 of assets per customer (with a limit of $100,000 on cash claims). But it does not insure against declines in market value, manipulation of stock prices, or losses through excessive trading by a broker. Nor, as a general rule, will it cover money lost in currency trading, hedge funds, or other securities that are not registered with the Securities and Exchange Commission. SIPC insures only against the bankruptcy of the brokerage firm or outright theft; if your broker steals up to $100,000 out of your cash account and absconds with it to Tahiti, you may submit a claim for that loss to SIPC.

SIPC plays hardball. The organization will replace assets that are stolen or are frozen when a brokerage firm goes bankrupt. But many victims of Bernie Madoff's investment scam were shocked, in late 2008, to hear that they would recover a potential maximum of only $100,000, not $500,000, from SIPC. In stating that it would deny larger claims, SIPC took the position that Mr. Madoff had not actually put his clients' money into securities and that, therefore, SIPC had no obligation to cover claims greater than the $100,000 ceiling for cash. SIPC later relented, but the incident was a useful reminder that this particular guarantee is not as comprehensive as many investors would like.*

Whenever you open a brokerage account, you will be bombarded by notices that the firm is a member of SIPC. Your broker may even tell you that your account is "SIPC-insured." SIPC coverage is certainly better than nothing. Just remember, however, that it has so many loopholes and limitations that it does not qualify as comprehensive insurance.

Backed by Uncle Sam

You're better off when you have a government guarantee. In the United States, that comes from the Federal Deposit Insurance Corporation (FDIC) for bank deposits and from the National Credit Union Administration (NCUA) for deposits (or shares) at credit unions.

These agencies are backed by the full faith and credit of the U.S. government. If a bank or credit union goes bust, the agencies will immediately seek to intervene, find a buyer for the assets held at the failed institution, and ensure that all accounts are transferred intact to the new bank.

*Jane J. Kim, "Burned Investors Won't Find Strong Safety Net," *Wall Street Journal*, December 17, 2008, http://online.wsj.com/article/SB122945750489411369.html.

If no buyer for the busted institution can be found, the FDIC or NCUA's insurance fund will preserve the value of depositors' assets. Since the agency was founded in 1933, no depositor has ever lost a dime on assets that were covered by FDIC insurance.

There are limits on government guarantees, too. These agencies insure your deposits against bank failure—not against other causes of disaster. If you keep Aunt Minnie's precious pearl necklace in a safe-deposit box and it disappears, Uncle Sam will not cover your loss. And if your local branch burns to the ground, the bank itself will probably ensure that you get your money back; but the federal government does not guarantee you against that kind of loss.

Federal insurance covers traditional bank deposits: savings and checking accounts, trusts, certificates of deposit, and money-market deposit accounts (*not* to be confused with money-market mutual funds, which are *not* insured!). Individual retirement accounts (IRAs) are insured—but 401(k) and other forms of retirement accounts are not. Nor is any other form of investment that you might buy through a bank or credit union: stocks, bonds (even those issued by the U.S. government), insurance, annuities, mutual funds. And insurance coverage is generally limited to the first $250,000 per registered account holder (cooperatives like a homeowners' association, for example, are covered up to

$250,000 total—not per member).* Finally, some state-chartered credit unions are insured not by the U.S. government but by a private insurance company.

Thus it always pays to double-check whether a bank or credit union that *claims* to be federally insured actually is. It's a snap to do this at:

www.fdic.gov/deposit/index.html

www2.fdic.gov/idasp/main_bankfind.asp (for banks)

www.ncua.gov/indexdata.html (for credit unions)

If a cash deposit carries a guarantee from the government, then a little extra yield is not necessarily a red flag. Some community banks or credit unions—especially smaller, well-run institutions eager to expand their customer base online—will pay legitimately higher rates in an attempt to attract more business. With the government insuring you against loss, why not capture some of those higher rates for yourself?

The main thing to guard against is a teaser rate, a fat yield that will not last. Before opening any account, make sure you have read all the fine print and asked the right

*Amid the financial crisis, the insured amount was temporarily raised to $250,000. The amount of coverage is scheduled to revert to $100,000 on December 31, 2013.

questions: Is the quoted yield net of all fees? Are there any penalties for early withdrawal? Are there any conditions or circumstances under which the quoted yield can be changed?

Two trustworthy web sites that offer links to banks and credit unions with the highest available rates are: http://bankdeals.blogspot.com/ and www.checkingfinder.com. (Another site, www.bankrate.com, also offers good information but is more commercial and harder to navigate.) Investors who are comfortable with online transactions can, in many cases, triple the yield on their cash by signing up for an Internet account with one of these institutions. Just remember: *Always* check independently to verify that the institution is covered by government insurance.

You can also boost the level of your deposit insurance with a nifty wrinkle called the "POD account." POD stands for "payable on death" and simply means that you have named at least one beneficiary who stands to inherit the account if you die. For each person you add as a beneficiary, you can pick up FDIC insurance coverage for another $250,000. Robert Ring of Boise, Idaho, used this technique. By adding his three children as beneficiaries of a money-market account, he secured FDIC coverage for every penny of his $300,000 account at IndyMac Bank—even though the institution went bust in July 2008.*

*Jane J. Kim, "Your Cash: How Safe Is Safe?" *Wall Street Journal*, Sept. 18, 2008, p. D1.

If you very carefully follow the FDIC's rules, you can make your safe money a little safer still.

Safe Bets

- Don't count on SIPC insurance to bail you out of your investment mistakes or every kind of dishonesty by a financial adviser.

- Do take the time and trouble to verify that your bank or credit union carries the insurance it is supposed to.

Chapter Six

Fixing Your Fixed Income

How to Stop Chasing Yield

ONE DAY ABOUT 2,050 YEARS ago, a heathen approached the great Jewish sage Hillel and dared him to explain all of Judaism while the heathen stood on one foot. Hillel replied: "What is hateful to you, do not do unto your neighbor. All the rest is commentary; now go and learn it."

After almost a quarter century of writing about the bond market, I can explain all you need to know about bonds while you stand on one foot:

Don't reach for yield.

You can put your other foot back down now, and let's see why those four words say it all.

What Is Yield?

Yield is simply a bond's interest income divided by the bond's price. Higher yield can come from larger interest payments, or from a lower bond price. (As price goes down, yield goes up.) When interest rates rise in the market, new bonds offer higher interest income—making older bonds less attractive. As a result, the yield on older bonds must rise if anyone is to want to buy them.

Many investors do not realize that higher current yield does not ensure higher future return. In fact, if interest payments are not stable or the bond might fail to pay income at all, a rising yield may be the first sign that trouble is brewing.

Why Buy Bonds?

Historically, bonds have tended to zig when stocks have zagged—thus providing a cushion for the bone-crunching roller coaster of the stock market. During the sickening crash of stock markets worldwide from October 2007 to

March 2009, stock-only investors lost 60 percent of their money—leaving them with only 40 cents left of every dollar they started with. Someone with a 30 percent position in bonds would have cut those losses almost in half—finishing with 63 cents on the dollar. And an investor with a 50–50 mix of stocks and bonds would have survived the most catastrophic bear market in decades with 78 cents on the dollar intact—damaged, but hardly devastated.

Another valuable—but seldom discussed—function that bonds serve is fighting deflation. Normally the cost of living rises almost relentlessly; year after year, you must live with inflation. But sometimes, the cost of living falls as the prices of most goods and services go down; that's called *deflation*. Because companies struggle to increase their profits whenever they cannot raise the prices of their products, the stock market tends to do terribly during deflation. And because the prices of whatever you are selling—namely, the wages for your labor—are also likely to fall, deflation can be miserable for many people. That's especially true for anyone who owes money, since if wages are falling you must work harder with each passing year to cover your fixed mortgage payments or other debts.

Deflation is good for bonds and bondholders, however. With each passing year of deflation, the fixed income from your bond will go further, buying more goods and services. Say you own a bond that pays $500 in annual interest. This year, that might cover three weeks' worth of grocery bills. If prices keep falling next year, you will still earn the same fixed $500 in bond interest, but thanks to deflation, it might cover almost a month's worth of groceries.

During the deflationary slog of the Great Depression, as the cost of living dropped an annual average of 8.6 percent from the end of 1929 through the end of 1932, stocks lost an average of 26.9 percent per year—while intermediate-term Treasury bonds gained 4.3 percent.

Since 2008, many financial pundits have worried about inflation rather than deflation. And inflation does seem more likely, given the way governments around the world have been printing money as if there is no tomorrow. But Japan has suffered roughly two decades of deflation even after implementing some of the same steps the U.S. government is now taking in response to the financial crisis.

If deflation does occur, bonds will help your portfolio survive.

More important than the financial cushion, perhaps, is the psychological cushion that bonds can provide. By helping to preserve your overall store of capital, a position in bonds can keep you from panicking out of stocks at the worst possible time. When losses on your stock portfolio are offset by gains or stability in your bond portfolio, you become less likely to bail out at a disadvantage when the stock market goes into a nosedive.

Bonding with Bonds

Should you buy bonds directly, or through a mutual fund or an exchange-traded fund (ETF)? Since individual bonds tend to be priced in denominations of $10,000 and you probably need at least 10 bonds in order to be safely diversified, investors who are investing less than $100,000 at a time should favor a traditional bond mutual fund—ideally a very low-cost index fund. Because many brokerages will charge a transaction fee to reinvest income dividends on an exchange-traded fund, a bond ETF is probably not worth considering unless you put in around $100,000. So, for most small investors, an indexed bond mutual fund is the best way to go.

How Fixed Income Can Come Unfixed

When you buy a bond (or a bond fund or an ETF), you become a lender, providing money to someone else: a company, a town or city, a state, a government agency, or a national government. In daily life, you would never make a loan to someone you didn't believe could pay you back. And getting paid back means getting 100 percent of the money you expect, exactly when you expect it—not a penny less or a day later. Remember the Second Commandment: *Thou shalt take no risk that is not most certain to reward thee for taking it.*

So what makes investors fall for the sucker pitch of "higher yield without higher risk"? Whenever you focus on the income generated by a bond or bond fund, it's easy to forget the basic math of bond investing:

Total return equals income plus—or minus!— any change in the principal value of the bond.

If a bond or fund has high current income, but the market value of the underlying investment is crumbling, then the total return may be negative. Imagine owning, in 2007, a mortgage-backed security paying 6 percent interest, or $600 on a bond that cost $10,000. Now imagine— it's easy if you try—that millions of homeowners are in danger of defaulting on their mortgages, jeopardizing the value of all mortgage-backed securities. So the market decides that your bond is worth only $6,000 instead of $10,000. For now, at least, your bond is still paying its $600 interest. What began as a 6 percent yield has now become a 10 percent yield ($600 in income divided by the $6,000 current market value of the bond). But you are not better off when you measure your total return. You have a 40 percent loss on the principal ($10,000 minus $6,000). Even factoring in the high current income, you have lost well over 30 percent on a total return basis—a nightmare for any investor who seeks safety.

But someone else, starting from scratch, might find this disaster attractive—especially in the search for current income. After all, the bond is yielding 10 percent, and (so far at least) that income has not dried up. And any broker or trader is unlikely to emphasize the negative total return; instead he will talk about how wonderful that income is. It's hard for the investing brain to resist the allure of a 10 percent yield *now*, when the risk of a loss will come home to roost *later*.

Yields on Steroids

Let's look at three classic examples of how Wall Street puts yields on steroids.

In the late 1980s and early 1990s, as interest rates came down and bond yields fell sharply, so-called option-income or government-plus funds became all the rage. At their peak, around 1988, these funds had gathered billions of dollars from tens of thousands of investors—many of them retired or elderly, who simply wanted a stable stream of ample income to supplement their pensions or Social Security. A standard portfolio of Treasury bonds or high-quality municipal bonds would have done the trick, but most of these people were pushed into reaching for higher yield by brokers who earned huge fees from the fund companies.

At their peak, when Treasury bonds yielded around 8.5 percent, many of these funds boasted yields of 10 percent to 12 percent. How do you get a 12 percent yield out of an 8.5 percent bond?

The government-plus funds used a strategy that managed to be both incomprehensible and stupid at the same time. I'll summarize the incomprehensible part by saying that they sold away the right to keep their long-term bonds if interest rates fell. In exchange, the funds got a short-term gusher of cash.* You may already see what made this strategy stupid. Why turn a long-term, durable source of steady income into a short burst of high income? And why turn lower interest rates into a source of higher risk?

Yet the brokers—who were paid as much at the moment of sale as most clients could hope to earn over the entire first year—insisted that these steroid bond funds were taking only "slightly" more risk and were sure to earn "much higher yields." And the funds spent millions of dollars a year on advertising that bragged about raising yields without sacrificing safety.

---

*The cash did not come from interest payments generated by the bonds, but rather from premiums generated by selling call options on the bonds.

But the yields were bogus. As interest rates continued dropping, the funds had to sell all their best long-term bonds below market value; the extra income disappeared, they took a loss on the bonds, and they could replace them only with more expensive bonds that offered less income.

Investors in these Frankenstein funds found that their yield kept dropping *and* the value of their accounts kept shrinking. Month after month after month, they took another battering. It was like falling in slow motion down an endless marble staircase with no clothes on. Some investors lost a third or more of their money, in the midst of one of the biggest bull markets for bonds of all time.

Another example is short-term world-income funds, which were all the rage in 1991 and early 1992. As interest rates dropped in the United States, fund companies raced to launch portfolios that invested in higher-yielding European securities and also speculated in foreign currency, furiously trading futures and options to profit from Europe's impending currency union. The Merrill Lynch Short-Term Global Income fund raised an astonishing $6 billion in 1991, making it one of the fastest-growing mutual funds ever. At the end of 1991, short-term world-income funds had more than $16 billion in assets and typically promised "the highest level of current income consistent with prudent risk."

Then, in September 1992, billionaire speculator George Soros "broke" the overvalued British pound, throwing the European monetary system into turmoil. Suddenly the smooth profits of 1991 turned into jagged losses; in 1992, the Kemper Short-Term Global Income fund lost 8.5 percent, the Merrill Lynch fund lost 3.3 percent, and the Pilgrim Short-Term Multi-Market Income fund lost 15.1 percent. Investors looking for high yield at relatively low risk could simply have kept their money in intermediate U.S. Treasury bonds, which gained 7.2 percent.

Another update of this age-old story played out in 2008. At its peak in mid-2007, Schwab YieldPlus had raked in more than $13 billion from investors eager to capture the holy grail of more yield and less risk. Its net asset value, or price per share, had stayed extraordinarily close to $10 for years, hardly ever wavering up or down. The fund boasted about its broad diversification across hundreds of different bonds, reporting in late 2007 that it had (among other investments) 46.2 percent of assets in mortgage-backed securities, 34.9 percent in corporate bonds, 7.9 percent in asset-backed obligations, and 7.6 percent in cash and preferred stock.

But a second look would have shown that this quest for high yield at low risk was doomed to end as badly as all the others. Diversification does not depend on how many investments you have; it depends on how different your investments are from each other. And nearly all the bonds in this fund depended on the mortgage and real-estate markets. Even though financial companies account for well under half of total corporate bond issuance in the United States, 79 percent of the fund's corporate holdings were issued by banks and other financial firms, including hundreds of millions of dollars' worth tied directly to mortgage and real-estate companies. Plus, the fund's industrial bonds included $210 million in debt from the nation's biggest home builders.

Far from being diversified, Schwab YieldPlus was a concentrated bet on the perpetuation of the real-estate boom. When the boom went bust, the fund went down with it—losing 35.4 percent in 2008, a year in which bonds overall gained about 5 percent.

Finally, consider the Oppenheimer Core Bond fund, which lost 36 percent in 2008. According to its own documents, the fund was intended to provide "income," "protection of principal," and "preservation of capital" by investing in intermediate-term bonds. Yet it chose weird ways to do so: The fund bought some of the riskiest bonds in the country, from issuers like American International Group, Citigroup, Ford Motor Company, General Motors, Lehman Brothers, and Merrill Lynch, and then sold credit-default swaps (CDS) on those same issuers.

By one estimate, the fund had put a third of its assets into selling CDS on its own troubled bonds. This was an extreme way of gambling that those bonds, which most investors had already decided could go bust, would turn out just fine. It was the equivalent of an insurance company offering fire-insurance policies only on buildings that are already engulfed in flames.

It is also what an investor should expect from any fund that told investors it would "provide competitive yields . . . with potentially less volatility."* You can have more yield, or you can have less volatility, but you cannot have both.

More yield and less volatility are what the great satirist Ambrose Bierce called "incompossible": two things that may exist separately but cannot exist together. And they violate the Second Commandment: *Thou shalt take no risk that is not most certain to reward thee for taking it.*

Investing is the art of the possible; it is not the black magic of the incompossible.

The High Risk of High Fees

The surest sign of a fund that may have to reach for yield is high annual expenses. Higher expenses must result in lower income for investors—unless the fund's managers

---

Source: Marion County, Oregon, court documents (www.oregon529network .com/Index%20Postings/090413%20Oppenheimer%20complaint.pdf), p. 17.

fatten up the yield first by taking extra risk. If they can pump the yield full of enough steroids, no one will notice how high the expenses are, and they will still be able to sell the fund to new suckers.

There's a simple way to protect yourself. First, refuse ever to buy a bond fund with annual expenses greater than 0.75 percent. Stick with super-low-cost bond index funds. Or apply my 1.5 percent rule. Use a standard data service like Morningstar (www.morningstar.com) to determine the average yield and average annual expense ratio for the category of fund you are interested in (intermediate-term bond, for example); add those two percentages together. Then note the yield and annual expenses of the particular fund you are investigating; take the sum of those two numbers. Now subtract the category sum from the fund sum. If the difference is greater than 1.5 percentage points, stay away. This is a simple way of spotting which funds may be so high-cost that they must take high risks.

Take What Bonds Will Give You

In any case, never reach for yield. Remember: It's total return—income plus or minus any change in value—that matters. A high yield will do you no good if the underlying value of the bond or fund keeps decaying.

A bond fund paying 5 percent in a 4 percent market is almost certainly on steroids. Funds can't ultimately yield more than the bonds they own, any more than you can get a gallon of milk out of a one-quart container. Funds whose names include "plus" and "ultra" might as well be called "minus." Anyone peddling promises of higher yield without higher risk is either a liar or a fool. And if you buy any fund with high expenses, its managers will probably have to reach for yield even if you know better than to reach for yield yourself. Take what the bond market will give you, and resist all urges—internal or from outside experts—to grab for more.

Safe Bets

- Avoid high-cost bond funds as if they were poison. They are.
- Never buy a bond or a bond fund without checking both its yield *and* its total return.
- Favor bond index funds at rock-bottom cost.

Chapter Seven

Stocks for the Wrong Run

Do Stocks Really Become Risk-Free If You Merely Hold Them Long Enough?

As an investor, what you believe determines what you do. And, over the past decade, millions of investors have come to believe that if you just hold on to stocks long enough, they become risk-free—safer than cash, incapable of losing money, and guaranteed to whip inflation.

These people were seduced by a historical fiction—the fantasy that stocks have always returned an average of 7 percent a year, after inflation, and never underperformed bonds over any multidecade period for more than two centuries. Therefore, went the myth, investors can remove all the risk from stocks simply by hanging on to them long enough. The darn things might bounce around a bit every few years, but if you just grit your teeth and close your eyes for a couple of decades, when you open your eyes again you'll be rich. One book even claimed that when investors finally all smartened up and figured out that stocks were riskless, the Dow Jones Industrial Average would immediately hit 36,000!

But myths have consequences.

Millions of investors sank vastly more of their families' financial futures into the stock market than they ever should have—and many of them took that plunge immediately before the worst crash in nearly eight decades. Investors who put 100 percent of their capital into the stock market in October 2007 had only 40 percent of it left by March 2009. They will now need a gain of 150 percent *merely to get back to where they started*.

How could stocks be riskless? By any sensible definition, *risk* means the chance that you might lose money. U.S. stocks lost 89 percent of their value between 1929 and 1932. In Japan at the end of 1989, the leading Nikkei 225 stock index was at 38,915.87; two decades later, it languishes below 10,000, a nearly 75 percent loss. Argentina, Germany, Italy, Russia, and Switzerland are some of the many other stock markets that, at one point or another, have had long periods of disappointing returns.

So how could anyone ever possibly have argued that stocks are risk-free?

The History of a History

In 1935, two economists, Walter Buckingham Smith and Arthur Harrison Cole, published a book called *Fluctuations in American Business, 1790–1860*. As part of their project, Smith and Cole combed through antique newspapers, looking at stock prices. They were searching for the biggest, most stable companies they could find: stocks that traded continuously and never went bust. For the years 1802 through 1820, Smith and Cole built a stock market index out of a grand total of seven such survivors, all banks: three in Boston, two in New York, and two in Philadelphia. By the time they got to 1835, they had found 27 railroad stocks, although Smith and Cole complained of "the paucity of available data" and readily admitted that their index had "some small gaps" that had "to be filled by extrapolation."*

Professors Smith and Cole never pretended to be building an index of the performance of the entire U.S. stock market. All they were trying to do was to see whether major stocks, in the nation's earliest days, fluctuated more or less in sync with the economy as a whole. Their answer, by the way, was no: "Variation in bank-stock prices clearly did not serve as a business barometer."

In 1994, Smith and Cole's data reappeared in the famous book *Stocks for the Long Run*, whose author, Jeremy Siegel, used them to make a case that stocks have outperformed bonds over long periods ever since the days when Thomas Jefferson was daydreaming about Sally Hemmings.

The Smith and Cole data may give us a very rough picture of the returns earned by those lucky people who invested in the exact seven banks that happened to survive

---

*Walter Buckingham Smith and Arthur Harrison Cole, *Fluctuations in American Business, 1790–1860* (New York: Russell & Russell, 1969, reprint of 1935 edition), p. 178. As the distinguished finance professor G. William Schwert noted in 1990, "Smith and Cole omitted most of the stocks for which they had collected price data. They chose stocks in hindsight to represent typical movements in the period. The sample selection bias caused by only including stocks that survived and were quoted for the entire period is obvious."

and the 27 very best railroads. But that's not what American investors actually owned.

By 1800, there were already at least 300 "joint-stock companies" that had sold shares to the public. The vast majority of these stocks never traded on the floor of any exchange. No records were kept; almost no stock prices survive. And investors lost money on many of these companies, most of which disappeared without a trace.*

Every era has its hot stocks. Today, it's clean technology and the Internet. Back then, it was canals and wooden turnpikes. In May 1792, two big canals sold stock to the public for the first time: the Western Inland Lock Navigation Co., a venture that proposed to dig a series of canals connecting the Hudson River to Lake Ontario, and

---

*Sometimes, nineteenth-century shareholders were "assessed" or required to add even more capital—often 10 percent or more of their original investments—just to maintain their positions. When such companies ultimately went bust, shareholders could thus lose *more* than 100 percent of the money they originally put up. While assessments were hardly universal, they happened often enough. In *The Gilded Age* (written in 1873 with Charles Dudley Warner), Mark Twain spoofs them in his description of a corrupt canal venture, the Columbus River Slack-Water Navigation Co. A contractor seeking to collect on his bills is told that the company will do him a favor by subtracting those amounts from the assessment he owes the company on his shares of stock! Our modern market at least ensures that unmargined investors can normally lose only 100 percent of their money on a stock. That's not how it used to be in the bad old days.

the Northern Inland Lock Navigation Co., which would
have connected Albany, New York, with Lake Champlain.
Small investors in New York City and Albany snapped up
shares in these two emerging growth companies—but both
ran dry.

And wooden turnpikes? Back then they were as hot
as the information superhighway was in the 1990s. In
every decent-sized town in New England, an entrepre-
neur was clearing a straight path through the woods to
provide greater speed and comfort to horse-and-coach
traffic—and to collect the tolls that would make his
shareholders rich. Unfortunately, competition was
fierce, only a few of these toll roads ever made money,
and by 1830 the advent of the railroad had doomed
them all.

Don't Know Much about History

So how many of these overwhelmingly popular—but dis-
mally unprofitable—investments are captured in the
returns of the so-called early indexes of stock performance? Not a single one. They're simply not there.

Here's the point. We don't even *know* how the investors in these stocks did. Many of these shares were never
traded on an exchange; they changed hands at a negoti-
ated price, with no paper records kept, over tankards of
murky grog in taverns all over New England and the

Middle Atlantic states. Nor is it possible to come within a country mile of estimating the dividends on early American stocks; the records have long since been lost. What we *can* be pretty sure of is that many investors in industries like wooden turnpikes, canals, steamboats, and the pony express lost plenty of money, as the tidal waves of technological change sweeping this country in the nineteenth century washed all those industries into oblivion.

Furthermore, entire stock exchanges disappeared without a trace. By 1865, the over-the-counter markets in mining stocks in New York alone were capitalized at $800 million ($10 billion in today's money). Nearly every penny of it went down the drain, and not one penny of that loss is reflected in the historical data so often cited.

What's Google Got to Do with It?

There's an even more basic problem with these early stock returns. Not only do we not really know how stocks performed while James Monroe or Millard Fillmore was president, but it's far from clear why we should care. What can we possibly conclude about the future performance of Exxon Mobil or Google based on stock returns from an era when people wrote with quill pens by the light of lamps filled with whale oil?

Other than not putting too much of your money into the stocks of canals or wooden turnpikes, it's hard to say what lesson you should draw from the financial markets of 150 or 200 years ago. Let's face it: The twenty-first century is probably not the best time to invest in such stars of yesteryear as steamboats, telegraphs, or importers of bird guano from Pacific islands.

Furthermore, it's not reasonable to conclude, from the flimsy and fragmentary evidence of early stock prices, that stocks have never underperformed bonds over multi-decade periods. The earliest stock-return numbers are unreliable—and unrepresentative of the returns investors actually earned.

It just so happens that one 30-year period in which stocks have *not* outperformed bonds is the period that ended in early 2009. By late 2007, millions of investors had become convinced that stocks were predestined to outperform bonds—at which point the stock market crashed so badly that all traces of outperformance were wiped away.

And that brings us to a series of paradoxes: What history does prove is that how risky stocks *seem*, and how risky they actually *are*, are inversely correlated. Once everyone thinks stocks have become risk-free, then price is no object; no matter how much you pay for them, stocks will seem sure to reward you. At that point, the market has to crash, since investors will no longer buy logic at any price.

In the aftermath, no one will want to own stocks—and those who do buy them will ultimately be rewarded richly for doing what their peers now regard as insane. And the buy-and-hold philosophy can work in the end only if there comes a time when most people no longer believe in it.

So history does not tell you whether to buy stocks. Price does, and psychology does. When everyone believes stocks have to be cheap at any price, then investors have lost their minds and are about to lose their shirts. But when the investing public believes that stocks are no longer worth owning after a crash, you should eventually be rewarded if you invest.

That's why the great investor Shelby Cullom Davis was right when he said, "You make most of your money in a bear market; you just don't know it at the time." The opportunity to buy stocks on sale, from people who have been heartbroken by the death of their beliefs, comes along only a few times in a lifetime.

The end of 2008 and the beginning of 2009 represented such a time. Stocks have since bounced back so far so fast that many of the bargains are gone. That means their future returns will likely be lower—not higher, as most investors now seem to believe.

Safe Bets

- Your own emotions are a decent guide to future stock returns: When you think gains will be great, they are likely to shrink. When you think the world is coming to an end, stocks are probably cheap.

- Don't believe anyone who tells you that stocks are certain to beat every alternative in the long run. That depends on how expensive stocks are today and how cheap other assets like bonds are.

- Invest as if stocks are likely—but *not* certain—to beat all other assets. Keep some money in bonds, cash, and real estate just in case they do better.

Chapter Eight

Rules for Stock Investors to Live By

Staying Out of Trouble in the Stock Market

HOW, THEN, SHOULD you invest in stocks?

First, learn from the legendary investor Benjamin Graham, who was Warren Buffett's teacher and the founder of modern financial analysis. Graham had three great insights:

1. You must focus not on stock price, but on business value.

2. You must understand Mr. Market.
3. You must maintain a margin of safety.

Let's take each in turn.

Stock prices change every few seconds during the trading day. But the value of a business changes, at most, a few times a year. In the short run, the price of a stock is affected by everything from how sunny it is today to what some blogger in Bulgaria says about one of the company's products. But in the long run, the price of a stock is determined by how much cash is generated by the underlying business. If the enterprise keeps creating more cash, then it becomes more valuable and the stock price will rise with it. And if the business does not grow more valuable, then nothing can keep the price of the stock up in the long run.

So stop spending all your time watching what the stock price is doing. Instead, learn as much as you can about the business. Would customers remain loyal even if the firm raised its prices? Do its competitors seem powerless against it? Does it generate more cash than it consumes? Can it finance its expansion without borrowing money? Are its employees loyal and happy? Are its managers fairly paid, but not overpaid?

If you buy any investment purely because its price has been going up, or sell it merely because its price has dropped, *then you are not an investor at all*. You are a spec-ulator, and your future gains will always be held hostage by the whims of the crowd.

Next, come to terms with Mr. Market. That's the nickname that Graham gave to the collective mood swings of investors. Graham asked you to imagine that you are the main owner of a private business in your community—a farm, a dry cleaner, a dental practice, you name it—and that every day one of your partners in that business, a man named Mr. Market, comes knocking at your door. Some days, he offers to sell you his stake for a ridicu-lously high price. Other days, he tries wheedling you into selling your stake to him at a ridiculously *low* price. Would you trade your stake with Mr. Market just because he asks you to? Or would you, instead, calmly tell him that you have no interest in trading a part of your busi-ness at a price that is either too high or too low?

Mr. Market is more than an image or a metaphor. He's real—he is the embodiment of the hundreds of mil-lions of investors and traders whose whims make daily stock prices look like the EKG chart of someone having a heart attack. You do not have to trade with these often-crazy people just because they ask you to. You must not let your view of a stock's (or an entire stock market's) value be determined by the glee or gloom of millions of strangers. In fact, Mr. Market's eagerness to trade with you is a signal that you should take no action at all without determining independently, using your own judgment, whether the price is right.*

Finally, preserve a margin of safety. Too many investors devote all their attention to figuring out the odds of being right. Every investor also needs to think about the odds of being wrong—and how to minimize the consequences if, indeed, your judgment of value turns out to have been mistaken. You must constantly ask yourself how much you can lose if you are proven wrong in the end, and you must invest only in opportunities that, on average over time, offer a better chance for profit than for loss. And you must diversify—by never putting too much of your money in one investment, no matter how sure you are that it will be a winner.

Graham offered one other profound idea. He divided all investors into two camps: "defensive" and "enterprising." The difference, Graham taught, is not in how much risk they seek, but rather in how much time and effort they are willing to devote to the work that investing requires. The defensive investor has no interest in spending hundreds of hours doing homework on stocks and funds. The enterprising investor, by contrast, willingly commits vast

*For a more detailed discussion of how to analyze investment value, see Benjamin Graham, *The Intelligent Investor*, updated with new commentary by Jason Zweig (New York: HarperBusiness, 2003).

amounts of dedication to his or her investing decisions. The enterprising investor can begin with Graham's principles and move on from there. The defensive investor can rely, even more simply, on the Three Commandments.

The Three Commandments

To Graham's three central principles, we can add the Three Commandments for extra guidance on how to add stocks safely to your portfolio.

~

The First Commandment: Thou shalt take no risk that thou needst not take.

From the First Commandment, it follows that you must not overinvest in the stock of the company you work for. Because it is the one stock you almost certainly know the most about, you may well feel more comfortable investing in it than in any other. That would be a mistake, as we saw in Chapter 3. You are already taking the risk of working for the company. You should not take the same risk twice by investing in it as well.

If you will have a known spending need on a certain future date—for example, tuition bills 12 to 15 years from now when your first grader will be in college, or a down payment on a house five years from today—then first count up all the savings you have already set aside for that goal. Next, see whether you can buy a low-risk bond that can get you there. Let's say you know you will need $12,500 seven years from now, and you have only $10,000 now. You might think you have to risk some of that money in the stock market, but you'd be wrong. If you put the $10,000 in a seven-year Treasury Inflation-Protected Security (TIPS) at its recent yield of 3.3 percent, you can be certain of having $12,500 on your target date.*

An online calculator like the one at www.nwcu.com/knowledge_center/calculators/compoundint.aspx is a quick way to check whether you need stocks at all in order to fund a specific goal by a certain date.

If the return on bonds is not high enough to get you to your goal, then your next step should be to save more. You cannot control the future returns of the financial markets. The stock market is not an automated teller machine (ATM) that exists to spit money out of a slot whenever you need some cash. In fact, the stock market doesn't know you exist, and it will not generate a high future return because you happen to need it.

---

*If you buy a TIPS bond directly from the government at www.treasurydirect.gov, you may incur annual income tax on "imputed income" as the bond's value automatically adjusts to take inflation into account. You could also consider a mutual fund like Vanguard Inflation-Protected Securities or an ETF like iShares Barclays TIPS Bond Fund.

If you raise your own rate of saving, you can make your money grow at 8 percent or 10 percent a year even when stocks do not cooperate with big gains. (For some practical suggestions on saving more, see Chapter 9.)

The Second Commandment: Thou shalt take no risk that is not most certain to reward thee for taking it.

Remember that stocks are not certain to outperform bonds and cash no matter how long you hold on. However, stocks are the simplest way to capture a share of the profits generated by businesses across society. Investing in stocks is like owning a small stake in the entire national (and even global) economy.

Why, then, do so many investors choose not to own the whole pie, but rather just some ragged slices here and there? Everyone thinks he knows something everyone else doesn't know. Yet somehow the irony of that is lost on most investors. You cannot buy a stock unless someone else is willing to sell it to you. One of you must be wrong. Who is it more likely to be: the person who already owns the stock and wants to get rid of it, or the one who hasn't even bought it yet?

Dazzled by their own knowledge and oblivious to the fact that other people are at least as knowledgeable, millions of investors move their money around every day, frantically elbowing each other aside trying to get a front-row seat on whatever they think is just about to happen next. Health care is bound to do well, so I'll buy a fund for that. Oil is going up, so I'll buy stock in Chevron. Banks are beaten up, so I'll buy a fund of financial shares. Global warming is getting worse, so I want "clean tech" and "green tech."

The end result is not a portfolio—an orderly set of investments that systematically covers all the bases—but a hodge-podge, a mishmash, a slop bucket full of market goulash.

And this result violates the Second Commandment: You are *not* most certain to be rewarded for taking on the risks of buying a fund full of medical stocks or one particular oil company or a basket of banks or any stock that's clean and green. After all, you might buy the wrong health-care fund. Chevron might not turn out to be the best oil stock. The basket of bank stocks might underperform the stock market as a whole. A technology that's even cleaner and greener may come along out of the blue. Furthermore, if you are investing for a lifetime, why would you want to run the risk that a particular fund manager—or corporate CEO—might not be around as long as you are? And hot hands go cold: If the manager's or CEO's performance has been good lately, it is likely to decay, often starting from the very moment you invest.

The risk you *are* likely to be rewarded for taking is the risk of owning all stocks. In effect, rather than betting on one roll of the dice, one spin at the roulette wheel, or a single hand at the blackjack table, you can own the whole casino.

You can do this effortlessly, cheaply, and reliably by buying a total stock-market index fund, a low-cost portfolio of all the stocks worth owning. This kind of fund is designed not to outsmart all the people who think they are smarter than each other, but rather to benefit from their collective wisdom. The best guess of what all stocks are worth is the price that all investors—buyers and sellers alike—place upon them. (No matter how crazy they may get from time to time, they are right more often than they are wrong.) An index fund simply buys and holds all the stocks in a market, giving you a permanent ownership stake and minimizing the risk that you own too much of some stocks and not enough of others.

This strategy cannot assure you of outperforming bonds or cash, even in the long run. But it does ensure that you will earn nearly 100 percent of whatever stocks do return.

The Third Commandment: Thou shalt put no money at risk that thou canst not afford to lose.

Many people invest not just to increase their wealth, but also because it's fun. Much the way recreational gamblers go to Atlantic City or Las Vegas and blow a couple of hundred dollars on the slot machines, others "play" the stock market.

There's nothing wrong with that, as long as you know you are playing, as long as you know the odds are against you whenever you play, and as long as you play only with money you can afford to lose.

You also owe it to yourself to get a realistic under-standing of the odds you face. Maybe, in search of the next Google, you want to buy initial public offerings (IPOs) of companies selling stock to the public for the first time. Well, don't be fooled by Google; it's the exception, not the rule. IPOs do outperform the stock market as a whole on their first day of trading (when you probably can't get any shares anyway). But over the long run, they underperform miserably, as you can see at finance profes-sor Jay Ritter's IPO web site at the University of Florida (http://bear.cba.ufl.edu/ritter/ipodata.htm).

So, if you're sure that ZygloWaxx is the next Google, first ask yourself: Why, out of the more than 8,800 com-panies that launched IPOs from 1975 through 2008, did so few of them turn out as well as Google? What reasons do I have to believe that ZygloWaxx will be different from the vast majority of IPOs? And what makes me so sure that the insiders who want to dump their ZygloWaxx shares on me don't know more about it than I do?

In short, an honest look at investing in IPOs should tell you that you can, and very well might, lose every penny you put in. If you still think the thrill of trying to hit the jackpot against lousy odds is worth it, then go ahead. But never gamble without knowing you are gambling. And never gamble without bracing yourself to roll snake eyes.

Finally, keep the Third Commandment in mind when you decide whether to invest in stocks at all. The stock market can destroy 60 percent or even 90 percent of your wealth in the wink of an eye. If you find that risk too painful to bear, then you should feel no shame or regret in staying out of stocks. You are the one who must live with your investing decisions, and you would be foolish to follow a strategy that you find psychologically painful. If, after the bear markets of the past decade, you feel that you cannot stomach investing in stocks, then you probably shouldn't. That would be violating the Third Commandment, and if anyone knows how much pain you can withstand, it's you.

If you do take this course of action, however, you could fall short of your savings goals unless you live a thriftier life.

Safe Bets

- Don't think stocks are a sure thing.
- Do follow Graham's rules and honor the Three Commandments.

Chapter Nine

Little Things
Mean a Lot

*How You Can Save More and
Make Your Money Go Further*

Americans, and citizens of many other countries, have forgotten how to save in recent years. First we came to regard the stock market as our piggy bank; if we needed a little spending money, surely we could always sell a few shares of stock or a bit of a mutual fund at a profit whenever we needed it. Then we viewed our houses as money machines that would always provide a surplus of cash on a moment's notice, since real estate "never goes down in value."

At least for now, all that has changed. People finally have again realized how important it is to save. After all, thrift was once one of the quintessential American virtues: Just think of Benjamin Franklin intoning, "A penny saved is a penny earned," or Abraham Lincoln reading Shakespeare by candlelight.

Our ancestors knew what we had forgotten until recently: Unless you save, you cannot make your wealth grow. It's much easier to tell ourselves that our horse will come in at the racetrack, or that we will win the lottery if we just keep playing 4-7-10-14-36-51, or that that some stock we heard about online is the next Google, or that we can simply use our credit cards to buy whatever we feel like today and pay it all back tomorrow . . . after our horse comes in at the racetrack. But Benjamin Franklin was right when he wrote: "Human Felicity is produc'd not so much by great Pieces of good Fortune that seldom happen, as by little Advantages that occur every day."

And the biggest of all "little Advantages that occur every day" is the simple act of saving money. That, in turn, requires you to become more mindful of where your money goes, and why, and whether you are spending it wisely and saving enough. You can't consistently and systematically cut your expenses if you don't know what they are.

As of 2007, the typical American household spent an annual average of:

$10,023 on rental or mortgage and other housing costs.

$3,465 eating at home.

$2,668 eating out.

$3,477 on utilities.

$2,853 on health care.

$2,698 on entertainment (including $987 on consumer electronics).

$2,384 on gasoline and motor oil.

$538 on public transportation.

$457 on alcoholic drinks.

$323 on tobacco.

$446 on furniture.

$1,881 on clothes.

$327 on shoes.

$140 on laundry supplies.

That's not a complete list, but it gives you a feel for both the necessities and the luxuries that we buy. We spend a lot on things we have to have (houses and health);

we also spend a lot on things we could, and perhaps should, live without (restaurant meals, booze, and smokes).*

Here are a few simple ways you may be able to raise your own rate of saving. Each will save you something; together, they will save you a lot.

Drive more efficiently. Don't gun your engine; avoid driving above 55 miles per hour whenever possible; set your car on cruise control for trips on long highways; use a smooth, light touch when you accelerate. Driving at 55 miles an hour instead of 70 will save you the equivalent of roughly 70 cents a gallon, which could easily put hundreds of dollars a year into your pocket.

Before you start your car, get your kids seated and belted, adjust your mirrors, put on your lights and do all your other preparations for driving. This will save you a few minutes' worth of gasoline usage every day. For the same reason, don't idle your car; if you know you will have to wait more than a couple of minutes, turn it off. If your car has a dashboard monitor that tracks your fuel efficiency as you drive, use it to train yourself into driving more economically. For more tips, see www.fueleconomy .gov/feg/driveHabits.shtml.

---

*The full list is available at: www.bls.gov/cex/.

Set your thermostat to 65 degrees in winter and wear a sweater. Before you go to bed at night, set it down to 60 degrees and use a second blanket on the bed. In summer, set the air-conditioning on 70 degrees, not 65. At night in the summer, if you are using a blanket instead of just a sheet, that's a sign that you are spending too much on air-conditioning. Depending on where you live, adjusting your home thermostat wisely could save hundreds of dollars annually.

If you live in an old house, make sure it is properly insulated and that windows, doors, chimney, and basement are properly sealed. Here, too, the annual savings can be in the hundreds of dollars. For more advice on saving on fuel bills, see www.energysavers.gov.

Walk or bike to work. If it's feasible, walking or biking, instead of driving or paying for a bus or train, could save you $5 a day, $25 a week, $1,250 a year.

Don't buy lunch every day at work. Instead, make and take your lunch. Better yet, pull together a brown-bag club with a few friends, with each of you bringing your own food plus something to share. You could save another $1,250 a year. And a few minutes of socializing will make you more productive the rest of the working day.

Cut back on dining out. Take a cooking class. For a couple of hundred dollars, you will acquire skills and recipes that you can use to make better food in your own home than most restaurants serve anyway—and you will be able to make it for a fraction of the price. According to the U.S. Bureau of Labor Statistics, the typical American household spends $6,133 a year on food, 44 percent of it on meals eaten outside the home. When you do go out, don't be afraid to skip an appetizer, share an entrée, or split a dessert. Always inquire how much the specials cost; the waiter won't tell you unless you ask. (Specials are typically no better than regular menu items, but they tend to be more expensive.) Don't order the second cheapest wine on the list, as many people do to avoid embarrassment. Instead, unabashedly order the cheapest one. It's usually almost identical in quality, so you might as well save the difference in price. If you like better wines, avoid the second most expensive bottle, which is often overpriced; get something slightly lower down on the wine list.

Quit smoking. At roughly $5 a pack, someone who smokes just two packs a day could burn through $70 a week, or more than $3,600 per year. Smoke like that for 20 years and, if you are still alive, you will have spent roughly $75,000. Quitting would save not only your life but a considerable amount of money.

Get your videos free from the local library. Depending on how often you rent, you could save $100 or more a year.

Use a clothesline instead of an electric or gas dryer to dry your clothes. If you do the wash twice a week, you could save $1 a week, perhaps $50 a year.

Put your fridge on ice. Before you open the refrigerator to take one thing out or put one thing in, pause for a moment to see if you can move several things in or out at once. Every time you open the door of the fridge, you make it work harder (especially in the summer)—so open it only when necessary. My guess is that a family that becomes more mindful about opening the fridge can save about 50 cents a week, or $25 a year.

Don't shop on an empty stomach. Walking into the supermarket when you are hungry can make you more inclined to buy food you don't really need. This is especially important if you are dieting; research has shown that willpower has its limits, and if you've resisted eating all day you will be especially prone to temptation. A light, nutritious snack before shopping could easily save you $100 a year, not to mention several hundred calories a week.

Avoid signing up for insurance, service contracts, or extended warranties on appliances and consumer electronics—especially on things like cell phones, which you will probably not lose or damage and, in any case, you are likely to use for only a couple of years at a time. The average American household spends an astonishing $1,110 a year on telephone services. While you're at it, get a cheaper flat-rate plan on your cell phone.

Above all else, manage your credit-card spending wisely. Leave your credit cards at home. Instead, pay with cash or checks. (Credit cards are essential for a few things, like online purchases, car rentals, or airline tickets, but you can do fine without them most of the time.)

And ignore the minimum payment on your credit-card bill, which the banks deliberately set at a very low level (typically around 3 percent of the total that you owe) to encourage borrowers to keep spending. Instead of paying the minimum they will accept, you should be paying the maximum you can afford. If you can't pay off the balance in full, then try to pay a substantial percentage of it, rather than a piddly dollar amount. If the minimum payment is $20, but you owe $774.84, see if you can pay $200 (a little more than 25 percent of the balance) or even $80 (about 10 percent of it).

A recent study found that 48.5 million Americans with active credit cards habitually pay only the minimum amount on their monthly statements, leading them to incur *$25.8 billion a year* in extra finance charges. Paying more than the minimum and curtailing your new purchases are the only ways you can climb out of the debt trap.*

Finally, shop around. You aren't stuck with the card you have; if you can find a better rate somewhere else, switch. You can compare rates at www.federalreserve.gov/Pubs/shop/survey.htm or www.bankrate.com/credit-cards.aspx. Many families could save thousands of dollars a year by getting their credit-card debt under control.

These are only a few ideas for economizing. You will have others, many of which will be better than mine. Send your favorite suggestions on saving to info@jasonzweig.com.

Having grown up on a rural farm in the recession of the 1970s, I happen to believe that spending less and saving more will lead you not only to a thriftier life but to better values. The great investor Benjamin Graham once defined happiness as "living well within one's means." Did he mean "*living well* within one's means" or "living *well within* one's means"? I think his ambiguity was intentional: He meant both. A thriftier life does not have to be about depriving yourself of necessities or even about forgoing all luxuries. It is simply about making sure that your priorities are in tune with your finances, that whenever possible you spend the most on the things that you

*Annamaria Lusardi and Peter Tufano, "Debt Literacy, Financial Experiences, and Overindebtedness," National Bureau of Economic Research working paper, March 2009, www.nber.org/papers/w14808.

enjoy the most, and that you become more mindful about what you get for your money. Always looking for value can, and should, be one of your values.

And it's high time everyone woke up to the fact that *save* and *safe* come from the same root word: the Latin *salvus*, which means uninjured, complete, healthy. If you do not save, you cannot make your money safe.

Safe Bet

- Pennies saved today turn into dollars down the road—the surest and safest way of all to increase your wealth.

Chapter Ten

How to Get Your Kids through College without Going Broke

529 Plans Can Be Part of the Solution—or Part of the Problem

IT HURTS TO LOSE YOUR OWN MONEY in the market, but losing the money you've set aside for your children is agonizing. Just look at what happened to so-called 529 plans.

At their best, 529s—named for the section of the U.S. tax code that permits them—are a safe, sensible, tax-free way to save for your children's college expenses. At their worst, they offer irresponsibly risky exposure to stocks and appallingly bad investments that can blow parents' money and students' dreams to smithereens.

All too many families have gotten the worst. Of the 3,506 options (including funds with different sales charges) in 529s tracked by the researchers at Morningstar in Chicago, 92.7 percent fell in value in the disastrous 12 months ending in February 2009—and 1,098 lost at least 40 percent.

Of course, the stock market was roughly cut in half over the same period. But college savers expected to do better, because the popular "age-based option" for 529s is supposed to protect them. Age-based plans should work like this: A young child's account starts out primarily in stocks and then, with each passing year, more money moves into bonds and cash. By the time the student hits college, less than 20 percent of the money should be at risk from the ravages of a bear market in stocks—limiting the potential damage from even an epic bear market to 10 percent or so.

Why is that important? Unlike retirees, who may stretch out their savings by spending less or working longer, students typically have a finite period—most often only four years—during which they spend their 529 savings. (The money in a 529 can be withdrawn tax-free only if it is used for the expenses of higher education.) Students in, or close to, college don't have the luxury of waiting for the stock market to recover.

Nevertheless, some states pushed students into stocks or out of cash—at the worst imaginable time. In April 2008, Oregon doubled the stock exposure in its "1–3 Years to College" portfolio to 40 percent. In January 2009, Virginia froze a prescheduled shift into cash, locking many 16-to-18-year-olds into keeping 25 percent of their money in stocks even as the market tumbled. In 2004, a 19-year-old in Rhode Island's aggressive age-based portfolio would have had 40 percent stocks, 30 percent bonds, and 30 percent cash. By 2008, the equivalent was 46 percent stocks (including real estate), 49 percent bonds, and a measly 5 percent cash.

The result, for many savers across the United States, was a fiasco. "We made the proper choice to protect our college investments by placing them in bonds, only to be destroyed by complete mismanagement," one reader of the *Wall Street Journal* lamented in an e-mail to me. "I started saving for my daughter when she was born in 1996," e-mailed another. "She has a 529 that has a negative return inception-to-date. In other words, the money would be worth more had I put it under a mattress."

A Failing Grade

Other 529 plans took too much risk all along. Several states, including Maine and New Mexico, offered 529 portfolios with zero allocation to cash for students over the age of 18. Even after North Carolina finally scaled back its risk in early 2009, a 17-year-old could still have 43 percent in stocks, real estate, and junk bonds. In Utah, students already in college could have 65 percent in stocks.

Says Mercer Bullard, a securities-law professor at the University of Mississippi: "In some states, the asset allocation for the 16-to-18-year-olds looks as if it was designed by the five-year-olds."*

Unfortunately, the states compounded their bad strategic decisions with even worse tactical choices. One of Maine's portfolios for students 18 or older consisted of the following Oppenheimer funds: 60 percent Limited-Term Government, 20 percent Core Bond, 10 percent Champion Income, and 10 percent International Bond. Gorging on mortgage derivatives, the first three funds lost 6.3 percent, 35.8 percent, and 78.5 percent respectively in 2008. The portfolio as a whole fell 22.5 percent over the 12 months ending in February 2009 (not including sales charges).

*Jason Zweig, "Did Your 529 Plan Blow Up on You?," *Wall Street Journal*, March 20, 2009.

The "Ultra Conservative" portfolio in New Mexico had 0 percent cash, 20 percent stocks, and 80 percent in two Oppenheimer bond funds; it dropped 22.6 percent in 2008. Some of the same funds blew up 529s in Illinois, Oregon, and Texas.

Assets in 529s, which peaked at $112 billion at year-end 2007, totaled $88.5 billion as of the end of 2008. Sadly, the public's faith in 529s appears to be based partly on a false premise: that the state government was watching out for them. Furthermore, the money managers who run the 529s earn much higher fees on stock and bond funds than on cash accounts, so they designed plans that kept the money locked into the assets that were most lucrative—for them!—for as long as possible. The result: higher fees for the money managers, higher risk for the college savers.

Getting a Better Grade

How should you go about protecting yourself? Start by visiting www.collegesavings.org and, from the "Compare 529 plans" tab, select your own state. Go to the web site of your state's plan(s); find the section usually labeled "Investment Options." Look up the choices normally described as "Age-Based." Follow the links until you come to a description of what proportion of the money is invested in stocks for children of various ages (often marked as "Asset Allocations").

Check first how much money a student who is 16 years old will have in stocks under this strategy. If it's 40 percent or more, the plan is probably taking too much risk. Next, look up the stock allocation for a student who is already in college—ages 18 and up. If that is more than 20 percent, then the plan is definitely too gung-ho.

It's hard not to conclude that, for many people, the typical 529 plan violates all of the Three Commandments.

What about the First: "Thou shalt take no risk that thou needst not take"? Most wealthy parents do not need to take on even more exposure to the stock market; since they can afford to pay for college anyway, it makes little sense for them to gamble in hopes of getting a few extra percentage points of return.

What about the Second: "Thou shalt take no risk that is not most certain to reward thee for taking it"? For middle-income and poor parents, the uncertainties of a heavy stake in stocks make a standard 529 a risk that may not be worth running. In the future, the stock market might keep up with the rate of inflation in college costs. But it might not.

And what about the Third: "Thou shalt put no money at risk that thou canst not afford to lose"? To scrimp and save for years, only to have those savings crushed by the irresponsible risks taken by the so-called experts you trusted, has been unbearably painful for many families. Savings, once gone, do not automatically come back.

Thus, for many—perhaps most—parents, a *prepaid* 529 plan may be a better choice than the standard 529 savings plan that has caused so much grief. In a prepaid plan, you invest a fraction of estimated future tuition, and the plan essentially guarantees you that it will keep pace with the rate of inflation in college-tuition costs. Instead of buying a stake in the fluctuations of the stock market, you are instead buying an interest in the future costs of attending college.

There are, of course, some exceptions. Grandparents may want to contribute to a standard 529 plan to supplement or complement what the child's parents are already saving. In most states, contributions to a prepaid tuition plan such as the Independent 529 Plan are not deductible for state income-tax purposes, while the state's own standard 529 savings plan usually is. (The Independent 529 prepaid plan covers only undergraduate tuition at private institutions, not room and board or any aspect of graduate education, while a standard 529 savings plan generally can be applied toward all costs of higher education.) In some states, prepaid tuition 529 plans may be closed to new investment, or local finances may be so shaky that there's reason to doubt whether the state government will be able to honor its guarantee of paying out the future value of the prepaid account. (The prepaid 529 plan in Alabama, for example, is no longer accepting new accounts as it struggles to honor its existing commitments.) For some or all of these reasons, a standard 529 savings plan may still make sense.

But as a general rule, depending on which state you live in and how bright your little scholars are, a prepaid tuition plan may be a better choice for you.

At least 19 U.S. states offer prepaid tuition 529 plans. You can learn more about them at www.college savings.com and www.independent529plan.org. Also, www .savingforcollege.com offers quick and useful comparisons of prepaid versus savings plans (although the site is commercial and not all the services are free).

A prepaid 529 plan offers the great advantage of hedging an uncertain future liability—your costs of educating your children—with a certain rate of return. Too many of the standard 529 savings plans still force you to manage that future risk by putting too much of your money into the stock market. For many people, that's not a chance worth taking.

Safe Bet

- Don't pick a standard 529 plan until you've ruled out a prepaid plan first.

Chapter Eleven

What Makes Ultra ETFs Mega-Dangerous

Why Daily Returns Tell You Nothing about Long-Term Future Returns

ALCOHOL ADVERTISEMENTS urge us to "drink responsibly." Cigarette packs are emblazoned with the surgeon general's warnings about cancer. And the firms that sell leveraged (or ultra) exchange-traded funds (ETFs) keep begging individual investors not to buy the things because they are designed exclusively for short-term trad-ing and can have wildly unpredictable long-term returns.

Nevertheless, roughly 13,000 people are killed in alcohol-related crashes in the United States each year, over 33 million Americans smoke at least once a day—and more than $1 billion a month poured into leveraged ETFs in 2008 and 2009, much of it from individual investors and so-called financial advisers who were searching des-perately for safety amid falling markets. Like the drinkers and smokers, the investors should have heeded the warnings.

Double Trouble

The attraction of leveraged ETFs is easy to explain.

Imagine you could read a print copy or online edition of the *Wall Street Journal* published exactly one year from today. You would be able to know, just by glancing at the headlines and the data in the "Money & Investing" sec-tion, how every major investment around the world would perform over the coming year.

Now imagine that someone told you about a fund (an ultra ETF) that could double or even triple the daily per-formance of a market index. That means you could buy a market that you know is going to go up 20 percent over the next year—and you could earn 40 percent, even 60 percent, on it.

That's not all. Leveraged ETFs also can do a double reverse or triple backflip. Funds of this kind ("ultra-short" ETFs) can earn two or three times the *opposite* of the daily return of an index—so, if you knew a market would go down 20 percent, the fund could go *up* 40 percent or even 60 percent.

Could anything ever be more of a no-brainer? Who in their right mind would ever settle for one dollar of profit when they could double or triple it with no effort whatsoever?

I hate to disappoint you, but getting your copy of the *Wall Street Journal* 365 days ahead of time is not the only element of fantasy here. You can't reliably double or triple your long-term return, either.

Welcome to the wacky world of ultra exchange-traded funds. Ultra ETFs are mega-popular. As of early 2009, there were 106 of them with $46 billion in total net assets; by most measures, they were the fastest-growing investment in America. Countless investors, and thousands of financial advisers, have bought ultra ETFs in hopes of doubling and tripling their money.

Others buy ultra ETFs for supposed safety. As one financial adviser e-mailed me in early 2008, "You and I both know the only sure thing is that the global economy is going to hell in a handbasket. It's irresponsible not to take defensive action. Safety first! That's why I'm protecting my clients' assets by building positions in ultra-short ETFs as the stock market crashes. Ultra-short ETFs are an incredibly powerful tool to protect a portfolio from falling values."

I read this adviser's e-mail shaking my head sadly, since it was clear that neither he nor his clients had the remotest idea that in the name of "safety" he was embarking on one of the most uncertain investing strategies on earth.

That's because these funds are perfectly predictable in the short run but impossible to predict for sure in the long run.

What a Difference a Day Makes

When you buy an ultra ETF, you can be sure what return you are going to get each day. An ultra ETF? Twice as much as the market! (A 5 percent gain in the index is 10 percent in my pocket.) An ultra-short ETF? Twice the inverse of the market's return! (A 5 percent loss for the market is a 10 percent profit for me.)

And that is exactly what will happen if—*but only if*—you hold your ultra fund for one day and no more. If, though, you hold on for more than a single day, then you may have just chucked your assets into Pandora's box.

Yes, you might hit the jackpot and double or triple your money. But it's also possible that you will make next to nothing, lose money, or almost get wiped out. The long-term returns of ultra funds are a wild crapshoot that can distort the returns of the underlying markets beyond recognition.

What accounts for this helter-skelter divergence between the short term and the long term? I want to make sure you see exactly how things go wrong with these funds, so please indulge me as I toss some numbers at you.

Picture an imaginary ETF that I will call the UltraShort SunStocks Fund, which seeks to deliver 200 percent of the inverse of the daily returns of the SolarTruth index of companies in the photovoltaic business.

Remember, the ultra-short ETF goes up twice as far when the index goes down—but it *also* drops twice as much when the index rises.

And there's the catch: Because the fund goes down twice as far on its bad days, it can wander farther and farther away from the underlying index over time.

Let's say the SolarTruth index goes up or down exactly 2 percent on alternating days. Here's what you'll experience over the course of just four days if you hold either the index itself or the ultra-short ETF that moves twice as far in the opposite direction:

	Starting Value	Change on Day 1	Value after Day 1	Change on Day 2	Value after Day 2	Change on Day 3	Value after Day 3	Change on Day 4	Value after Day 4
Index	$100.00	−2%	$98.00	+2%	$99.96	−2%	$97.96	+2%	$99.92
Ultra-short ETF	$100.00	+4%	$104.00	−4%	$99.84	+4%	$103.83	−4%	$99.68

Each day, the ultra-short ETF did exactly what it was supposed to do, delivering double the opposite of the index's return on that day. But it did not—repeat: *not*—do that for the four-day period as a whole. The index lost 0.08 percent from start to finish, so you might have expected the ultra-short fund to deliver a 0.16 percent gain. Instead, it went down 0.32 percent—losing twice as much as you would have guessed it would go up!

The longer you hang on to one of these funds, the more impossible it becomes to predict the result you will get.

Remember, the ultra-short ETF turns each daily loss by the index into twice as large a gain. (That's what makes people think it's a good hedge against the risk of falling markets.) But it also turns each daily gain by the index into a *loss* that's twice as big. By doubling down on its bad days, the ultra ETF keeps falling further behind. Doubling up on its good days cannot suffice to close that gap. Over periods of months and years, the ultra ETF may end up delivering returns that don't even come close to what you would expect.

Upside Down and Inside Out

Over the 12 months ending in July 2009, 55 percent of leveraged ETFs and more than 85 percent of ultra-short ETFs turned their investors inside out—delivering long-term losses when they should have produced gains, and gains when they should have produced losses.* More than half the time, investors got the exact opposite of what the daily returns promised.

Just look at this actual example. If, at the beginning of 2008, you had decided that oil was overpriced, you would have been proven right: The Dow Jones index of U.S. energy stocks lost more than 37 percent for the year. The ProShares UltraShort Oil & Gas ETF (trading symbol: DUG) is designed to deliver twice the inverse of that index's return. So did DUG go up 74 percent in 2008? *Au contraire*: It *lost* 9 percent! For a brief shining moment in the fall, it delivered big gains, but if you blinked you missed them. Furthermore, it added insult to injury: Not only did DUG dig you into a hole, but it paid out a short-term capital gain of $6.06 per share, meaning you had to pay a tax bill on top of your losses.

Likewise, emerging markets fell by 49 percent in 2008. If you'd bought the ProShares UltraShort Emerging Markets fund, however, you would not have gained twice the opposite, or 98 percent; you would have lost 24.9 percent. Real estate fell 40 percent in 2008, but the ultra-short real-estate fund wasn't up 80 percent; it went down 50 percent. And Chinese stocks fell 48 percent in 2008,

*Eleanor Laise, "Subpoenas Put Pressure on ETFs with Twist," *Wall Street Journal,* August 1, 2009, B1.

but the ultra-short China fund didn't gain 96 percent; it lost 53.6 percent. In each of these cases, if you had correctly predicted that the underlying market was due for a fall, *you would have lost your shirt anyway.*

Look at what happened to Stewart Gregg, an investor who e-mailed me with the sad tale of his own misadventures with ultra ETFs. "In early November [2008]," he told me, "I was very concerned about a spreading collapse in the stock market." So Mr. Gregg bought the ProShares UltraShort Dow 30 fund (trading symbol: DXD) to capitalize on what he was convinced would be the crash to come. And sure enough, over the next four months, the Dow Jones Industrial Average fell 6.5 percent. So did DXD gain 13 percent? No: It went *down* more than 6 percent and slapped Mr. Gregg with a whopping short-term tax bill to boot. Thus Mr. Gregg was precisely right—and yet ended up getting pounded anyway.

Embittered by his experience, Mr. Gregg calls ultra-short ETFs "toxic, unpredictable derivative securities dressed up as funds." For traders who hold for one day or less—or for anyone who wants to go to the trouble of frequent trading to adjust their exposure—these funds are fine. For investors, they are a disaster.

Ultra ETFs do exactly what they should do in the short run—and often what almost no one who owns them expects them to do in the long run. Tragically, thousands of investors and an embarrassing number of so-called financial advisers think they can use ultra ETFs as a long-term tool for managing risk and bolstering the safety of their portfolios.

For short-term traders, ultra ETFs are terrific tools that can control daily risks and capture explosive momentary changes in the markets. But you wouldn't—and certainly shouldn't—be reading this book if you are a short-term trader.

If you're a long-term investor seeking safety, rather than put one of these things in your portfolio, you'd be better off taking out your contact lenses with a pair of pliers or trimming your toenails with a chainsaw.

Safe Bet

- Don't invest in leveraged and inverse ETFs. Leave them to professional traders.

Chapter Twelve

Hedge Fund Hooey

~

Is This Really How the Smart Money Gets Even Richer?

IMAGINE THAT YOU GIVE me $1 million. I will take it off your hands for one or two years, and if you want any of it back in the meantime, you can't have it. Nor will I tell you anything about what I'm doing with your money; you will just have to guess what I'm up to. I will keep 20 percent of any gains, and I'll also take 2 percent of your capital for myself every year, even if there are no gains. It's a classic case of "heads I win, tails you lose."

That doesn't sound very appealing, does it?

But this is a hedge fund run specifically for "sophisticated investors" like you. And not just anybody who happens to have $1 million can get in. You have to be invited to participate, and I'm inviting you. That puts you in the company of some of the smartest and wealthiest people in the world, who have already entrusted billions of dollars to me.

Suddenly it doesn't sound so bad, does it?

I don't actually run a hedge fund, and I don't want your money. But this fictitious example may help you understand what makes hedge funds so seductive and, potentially, so destructive.

You might wonder why little old you would ever need to know about hedge funds. Aren't they purely toys for the rich?

Not really. If you and your spouse jointly earned at least $300,000 in each of the past two years, and if your net worth (including your house) is over $1 million, you're what many people would call upper middle-class—and what a hedge-fund marketer would call a prime target. Furthermore, increasing numbers of mutual funds and exchange-traded funds (ETFs) are either mimicking hedge-fund strategies or otherwise bringing hedge funds to Main Street. The pitch: These things go up when stocks and bonds go down. And the marketing drumbeat gets louder every year. But there's more to the story than a simple tale of diversification.

Why Sophisticated Investors Are Like Jumbo Shrimp

Many years ago, the great comedian George Carlin popularized the search for oxymorons, those absurd pairs of words that have no business being put next to each other, like "jumbo shrimp" and "United Nations." In December 2008, Bernie Madoff put the silliest of all financial oxymorons into the spotlight: "sophisticated investor."

Madoff is the legendary Wall Street trader and founder of Bernard L. Madoff Investment Securities LLC, which attracted more than $13 billion from Banco Santander of Spain, the International Olympic Committee, economist Henry Kaufman, Royal Bank of Scotland, moviemaker Steven Spielberg, the endowments of Tufts and Yeshiva Universities, and media mogul Mortimer B. Zuckerman. These sophisticated investors—along with many of the world's leading experts on hedge funds—were lured by Madoff's long track record of silky-smooth returns even in the roughest of markets.

But in 2009, Madoff went off to federal jail to serve a 150-year sentence for securities fraud, a Ponzi scheme that paid off old investors with the money it took in from new ones.

Madoff is not alone, of course. Earlier, trader Samuel Israel III and his Bayou funds raised several hundred million dollars from investors in what the Securities and Exchange Commission alleged to be a massive fraud.

Even when hedge funds may not be stealing money outright, they still can have the same effect on your wealth as a sledgehammer coming down on a porcelain teacup. In 2006, the Amaranth hedge fund lost roughly $6 billion, or about 50 percent of the assets its investors had entrusted to it, in three terrifying weeks.

Hedge funds are typically marketed for their supposedly exclusive ability to generate higher average returns than you could get from the kinds of investments any old slob can buy.

To which you should say: average, schmaverage. The numbers you hear bandied about are full of baloney, for several reasons, three of which are:

1. **Survivorship bias.**

    When hedge funds go out of business, they disappear from databases of performance. Which funds tend to go out of business? The lousy ones, of course. So, when they disappear, their rotten track records are erased with them. The average return includes only the winners, or the survivors; the losers no longer taint the historical record.

2. **Backfill bias.**

The managers of hedge funds wait to see which portfolios are the pick of the litter, then quietly euthanize the losers without ever having reported their existence. The winning funds go into public databases of performance only after they have privately proven to be winners. The averages are thus inflated by the returns on funds that spent most of their lifetimes closed to outside investors.

3. **Look-ahead bias.**

To demonstrate the superiority of their strategy, fund managers back-test it against a benchmark like the Standard & Poor's 500-stock index as it exists today. Many of the stocks in the index today were not there five or ten years ago; and many of its members from five or ten years ago are no longer included. The only way to be sure a particular approach would have beaten the S&P 500 over time is to measure it against the exact constituents of that benchmark over the entire period— something that managers almost never do.

Altogether, the return of the average hedge fund may be overstated by a shocking margin: as much as eight percentage points per year.*

How could it be otherwise? How could hundreds of hedge-fund managers, all charging obscenely high fees and competing fiercely against millions of other investors, somehow manage to beat the market as a group?

Of course, not all hedge funds are bad. A few, including the Quantum funds founded by George Soros and the Renaissance funds run by James Simons, have a long record of robust returns.

But the average hedge fund cannot be better than average. And the worst can lose astounding amounts of money in the wink of an eye.

In short, hedge funds are like the little girl who had a little curl: When they are good, they are very, very

---

*Nolke Posthuma and Pieter Jelle van der Sluis, "A Reality Check on Hedge Fund Returns," http://papers.ssrn.com/sol3/papers.cfm?abstract_id=438840; Jenke ter Horst and Marno Verbeek, "Fund Liquidation, Self-Selection, and Look-Ahead Bias in the Hedge Fund Industry," *Review of Finance* 11 (2007): 605–632; Roger G. Ibbotson and Peng Chen, "The A,B,Cs of Hedge Funds: Alphas, Betas, and Costs," http://papers.ssrn.com/sol3/papers.cfm?abstract_id=733264; Harry M. Kat and Gaurav S. Amin, "Welcome to the Dark Side: Hedge Fund Attrition and Survivorship Bias over the Period 1994–2001," http://papers.ssrn.com/sol3/papers.cfm?abstract_id=293828; Burton G. Malkiel and Atanu Saha, "Hedge Funds: Risk and Return," *Financial Analysts Journal* 61, no. 6 (November–December 2005): 80–88.

good, and when they are bad, they are horrid. It's simply a myth that you can't have a complete portfolio without them.

Are You an Oxymoron?

The biggest dirty secret of the so-called sophisticated investors who invest in hedge funds is that their due diligence often goes undone.

In 2005, two surveys of institutional experts on hedge funds found that while 56 percent felt their boards of directors could prudently "fulfill their fiduciary responsibilities," 67 percent did not believe they had all the necessary tools to "measure, interpret, and manage the risks." In other words, at one and the same time, *We will manage other people's money as carefully as if it were our own*, but *We're flying by the seat of our pants.**

And in late 2007, the Greenwich Roundtable, a nonprofit that researches alternative investments, conducted a survey of investors who collectively oversee more than $1 trillion in assets. Asked how they conduct due diligence of hedge funds, more than two out of three investors in the survey reported that they follow "an informal process" at least some of the time. More than 19 percent

*Christine Williamson, "Asset Class Draws Rave Reviews from Attendees at Workshops," *Pensions & Investments*, March 6, 2006, 28.

"always" evaluate funds informally, rather than using a standardized checklist or analytical procedure.

Remarkably, 6 percent of these sophisticated investors do not always read the prospectus before committing money—the equivalent of an airline pilot neglecting to look at the flight plans before taxiing the plane onto the runway for takeoff.*

Doing Your Due Diligence

Fortunately, you can learn from the mistakes of Bernie Madoff's victims and other sophisticated investors. Here's how to avoid getting clipped by a hedge fund.

Start with this basic rule: Never invest on word of mouth or reputation alone. No matter who brings you the hottest investment tip of the century, even if it is your best friend or your spouse, your answer must always be exactly the same: "I have a standard checklist of criteria that every investment has to meet. I never buy anything without filling in the checklist first."

If the person tries to cajole you with an "Aw, c'mon" or "You don't want to miss out," stand your ground. After all, if it's really such a great investment, it will surely stand up to greater scrutiny. In fact, if it is a great investment,

---

*"Survey of Due Diligence Practices among Investors in Alternative Investments," Greenwich Roundtable and Quinnipiac University, 2007.

then the more you learn, the more you will like it. How could anyone argue otherwise?

What follows is a simplified version of the kind of due-diligence questionnaire that would have kept anyone from investing with Bernie Madoff—and virtually all of the major hedge-fund blowups of the past few years.

You can apply much of it to any kind of investment, not just hedge funds or other exclusive offerings meant only for sophisticated investors.*

- Do the returns seem both realistic and sustainable? Does the firm admit to past periods of underperformance and disappointment? (Or does it claim suspiciously smooth returns, enormous margins of outperformance over the market as a whole, or a mysterious lack of losses?)
- Has someone explained to me, in terms I can actually understand, how the past returns were generated? What is this firm's edge? How, specifically, does it outperform the competition?
- What reasons do I have for believing that future returns should be comparable? If these returns are so attractive, why isn't everyone else trying to capture them, too?

*I thank Stephen McMenamin and the Greenwich Roundtable for their help in crafting a simplified due-diligence checklist.

- Will the firm running this fund tell me about all the other funds it has launched, including its losers?

- Did this fund earn most of its return when it was small or closed to outside investors? If so, why should it do well now that it is big and taking in anybody with a pulse?

- Have the returns been audited by an accounting firm I have heard of?

- Does the fund trade through an independent broker-dealer? (Or does it route its trades through an affiliated firm that provides another way for the fund's managers to line their own pockets?)

- Are the assets held in safekeeping, or custody, by a major bank like State Street or Bank of New York Mellon?

- Who else has tried similar strategies in the past and failed? What has this fund learned from other people's mistakes? How much money, and when, has it lost on its own mistakes? What conditions could make it lose money again, and how much?

- What role would this fund play in my overall portfolio? How might it complement—or be a decrement to—the other investments I hold? Did its worst past performance coincide with periods of poor returns on my other holdings?

- Who is responsible for implementing this strategy? Does the firm have enough staff to support all aspects of the operation? (Or is it overreliant on a few people, or even one person?)

- Can I meet the No. 2 person in the organization? What is the succession plan in case the founder(s) no longer can function?

- Does this fund depend on leverage, and what would happen if the firm could no longer borrow?

- What rate of return would the fund have earned in the past if it had been unable to use any leverage? How much would it have earned at 50 percent of its customary leverage?

- Who are the other investors in this fund? If any of them face a liquidity crisis elsewhere and have to yank out their money, what would happen to mine? Do any other investors have "side letters" or preferred redemption terms?

- If the fund had to sell everything it owned, where would the securities trade and who would price them? How are those prices independently validated?

- When can I access my money by redeeming my holdings? How much notice do I have to provide in order to get my money out? Has the fund ever suspended redemptions? Why? For how long?

- Will there ever be "calls," or requirements for me to put up additional capital?

- Can I trust the people running this fund? Have I done a background check on their personal and professional history?

- Have I read every page of the investment adviser's Form ADV (www.adviserinfo.sec.gov), searching carefully for any legal and regulatory problems or conflicts of interest?

- How is the firm paid? Do its fees not give it an incentive to take excessive risks? Do its employees invest their own money alongside mine? What percentage of their net worth is in the fund? If they sell, will they tell me? Are they charged the same fees and subject to the same restrictions as I am?

- If I lose every penny I invest in this fund, will I have enough left elsewhere?

Use a checklist like this and you will keep yourself safe from the temptation to fling your dough at the first hedge fund that comes along and flatters you with talk of how sophisticated you are.

On the other hand, if you invest with anyone who claims never to lose money, reports amazingly smooth returns, will not explain the strategy used, and refuses to disclose basic information or discuss potential risks, you're not sophisticated. You're an oxymoron.

Safe Bet

- Due diligence is called "due" for a reason. Do it!

Chapter Thirteen

Commodity Claptrap

*Will Hard Assets Make You
Rich, or Are Promoters Hoping
You're Soft in the Head?*

IN THE DESPERATE SEARCH for something—anything—that will go up when U.S. stocks go down, investors have been stampeding into gold and other hard assets. In the first half of 2009 alone, the StreetTracks Gold Trust (GLD), an exchange-traded fund that seeks to capture the returns of gold bullion, took in $11.9 billion in new money, or an average of $95 million a day. Launched only at the end of

2004, GLD has grown explosively; at $34 billion, it is one of the largest funds in the world.

Most of the money pouring into gold and other commodity funds is motivated by the belief that hard assets will hold up when the economy goes soft and when inflation takes off. Unfortunately, this belief does not hold water.

Born in Babylonia

What are commodities? Unlike stocks or bonds, which are indirect claims on the assets of companies or governments, commodities are themselves *things* that can be traded: Some come out of the ground (like gold, crude oil, or natural gas); some come from farms (cattle, soybean, or hogs); and some come from human ingenuity (interest rates, foreign currencies, and stock or bond indexes).

Trading in commodities is much older than trading in stocks and bonds. To insure themselves against a collapse in market prices, farmers in ancient Mesopotamia traded futures contracts—agreements to buy or sell commodities at a fixed price on a known date in the future—approximately 4,000 years ago.

If a farmer along the banks of the Euphrates River could get someone to agree to pay him today's price for barley for next year's harvest, then the farmer had locked in or put a floor under the price. If the price for barley

went down over the coming year, the farmer was protected, since the counterparty to his trade had essentially
sold him insurance against just such a drop in price.

Meanwhile, the counterparty had also bought protection: If the price of barley went up, the farmer still had to
deliver it to the purchaser at the price they had originally
agreed to in the futures contract.

The producer hedged against a fall in prices, the consumer hedged against a rise in prices, and the commodity
changed hands between them. The farmer gave away some
of his upside (if prices went up, he could no longer raise
his selling price) but got rid of all of his downside (if prices
fell, he was guaranteed to receive the higher price specified in the contract). The counterparty also gave away
some of his upside (if prices fell below today's level, he
could no longer buy barley at the new cheaper price) while
eliminating his downside (if prices rose, he was guaranteed
to receive the lower price specified in the contract).

Thus, no matter what happened to market prices,
both parties got what they wanted: a little insurance
against a big surprise. The traders in the markets of
Mesopotamia knew full well that every trade had one winner and one loser, and that insurance can only limit your
losses if you also agree to forgo some of your gains.

In short, these people who worshipped idols, rode on
donkeys, and recorded their trades on clay tablets appear

to have understood what they were doing better than many of the investors and financial advisers who are barging into commodity speculation today.

Inflation Fixation

The constant refrain of commodity bulls as they paw and snort their way over the landscape is that hard assets will protect you against inflation.

If you push back, however, the argument falls apart.

Gold tripled in value between 2002 and 2009, brushing $1,000 an ounce in 2008 and 2009. What the bulls don't tell you is that, adjusted for inflation, gold was around $2,200 an ounce back in 1980! Meanwhile, the cost of living for a typical American had risen roughly 175 percent over the same period.

Oil went from roughly $30 a barrel in 2004 to more than $130 in 2008. What the bulls don't tell you is that, adjusted for inflation, oil prices at their peak in 2008 were no higher than they had been in 1864!*

If you point out these inconvenient truths, the commodity bulls will dust themselves off and come right back from another angle. Gold has done far better, they insist,

---

*Oil prices peaked in July 2008 at $145.29 a barrel; in 1864, oil fetched $12 a barrel; www.measuringworth.com/calculators/uscompare/result.php shows that the value of $12 in 1864 is between $140.78 and $169.64 in today's dollars.

when measured in currencies other than the U.S. dollar. But for anyone who lives in the United States or any of the many countries whose currencies closely track the dollar, why should that matter? If gold has held up well against the Albanian lek or the Myanmar kyat, who cares (unless you happen to live in Albania or Burma)?

As for oil, the bulls will tell you that we are running out of it—that petroleum reserves are being drained worldwide, and that the rapid growth of India and China will consume oil faster than the world can pump it.

But humans are ingenious and adaptable. By the 1850s, whales had been hunted almost to extinction; how else could people fill their lamps with the whale oil that was essential to light their homes and offices? Then, in 1859, Colonel Edwin Drake hit a gusher of petroleum in Titusville, Pennsylvania, and before long crude oil was everywhere, a seemingly inexhaustible source of cheap energy.

If the price of crude oil goes up again, people will use less of it. And the world's brightest engineers and scientists will redouble their efforts to make crude oil obsolete.

The Resource That Never Runs Dry

A bet on an inevitable long-term rise in the price of oil— or any other commodity—is a bet against the infinite resourcefulness of human nature. Is that a bet you want to take?

In 1977, Atlantic Richfield Company, a leading oil producer, paid $700 million to buy Anaconda Copper. With oil prices softening after the peak during the Arab embargo of 1973 to 1974, Atlantic Richfield's executives wanted to diversify into a commodity they felt was more certain to go up in price. Copper then traded at about 60 cents a pound. But 1977 was also the year that the first functioning fiber-optic telephone cables were installed. Today, most telecommunications signals around the world travel not along copper wire, but rather along fiber-optic cables made from fused silica—which, as a glorified form of sand, is almost as cheap as dirt to produce. Today, copper trades at about $2 a pound—no more, after inflation, than it cost in 1977.

The history of commodity prices resembles a downhill ski run: It is full of little bumps and rises, but they are the exception, not the rule, and you would be foolish indeed if you let a few moguls fool you into thinking that you are moving uphill instead of down.

Insuring Failure

Imagine a world in which every commodity producer—farmers who grow corn, energy companies that drill for oil, mines that produce copper and coal—wanted to insure against a fall in future prices. And now imagine that you expected prices of those things to rise.

So if prices go up, the value of your futures contracts will, too, enabling you to make out like a bandit. End of story, right?

Wrong.

You've overlooked something. The producers of all the commodities want to insure against a fall in prices. But the *consumers* of those same commodities want to insure against a *rise* in prices. To give just one obvious example, oil companies like Exxon Mobil don't want the price to go down. But giant chemical companies like DuPont, which spend billions of dollars a year buying oil, don't want the prices to go *up*.

In other words, DuPont wants insurance against the same risk you are trying to profit from: higher prices.

Do you suppose DuPont hasn't already thought of this?

Trust me: DuPont, and every other major consumer of every other major commodity, has been hedging exactly like this for decades, often for centuries. Coca-Cola hedges against a rise in the price of corn syrup, Alcoa hedges against a surge in the price of aluminum, the Hershey Company hedges against the hazard of rising cacao beans prices.

The conventional wisdom about commodities is that you can make money merely by buying them and hanging on until prices soar; inflation alone will make you rich. But this belief ignores the fact that the industrial consumers of commodities are in the market every day, buying them in stupendous quantities, to insure against their own risks.

If you buy a small amount of insurance only after giant consumers have moved to buy theirs, you enter the market after the price of insurance has already been driven sky-high by bulk demand. (At such moments, as professional commodities traders know, you are much better off selling insurance than buying it!) As a result, you end up paying such a high price that you may lose money on your commodity investment even if your predictions about the future turn out to be true.

Since the value of insurance is a function of how much you have to pay for it, a buy-and-hold position in commodities can't possibly make sense. To buy and hold commodities permanently is mindless. And most people lack the expertise to trade them over the shorter horizons that are necessary to capture the imbalances of supply and demand.

There is money to be made in commodities—but most of it will be made by direct producers and industrial consumers, who hedge in vast volumes. Much of it will be made by professional traders. But almost none of it will be made by financial planners and stockbrokers—or their clients—who do not understand that the buyer who is last in line is guaranteed to get the lowest return. The only thing these people have insured is failure.

Safe Bets

- Insure against inflation with Treasury Inflation-Protected Securities (TIPS) or by buying stock in the industries that will do well when inflation makes your own industry suffer.

- For most people, commodities are too risky and expensive to try at home.

Chapter Fourteen

Spicy Food Does Not Equal Hot Returns

*What's Wrong with the Belief
That Emerging Markets
Must Outperform*

BEHIND THE WORLD'S HOTTEST markets is a cold truth many investors don't want to hear.

It has become investing gospel among everyone from strategists at Goldman Sachs to the guy behind the counter at your local diner that emerging markets are bound to outperform the U.S. stock market for decades to come. The biggest of these developing countries already have a nickname that makes them sound as if they should constitute the building blocks of your portfolio—"BRICs," or Brazil, Russia, India, and China—and their economies are growing two to three times faster than those of the United States and Europe. With such high economic growth today, how could their stock returns *not* be higher tomorrow?

And lately the stock markets in those countries have been hotter than a peck of habanero peppers. In the first half of 2009 alone, the MSCI Emerging Markets index gained 45 percent, versus 9 percent for the United States.

And investors have noticed, pouring $10.6 billion into emerging-markets mutual funds in the first half of 2009, or more than 34 times the total they added to U.S. stock funds. The iShares MSCI Emerging Markets Index fund is now the fourth biggest of all exchange-traded funds, with $30.8 billion in assets.

Investors are stampeding to capture the stunningly high growth of the developing world, especially with the U.S. economy shriveling. In the second quarter of 2009, China's economy officially grew 7.9 percent, while the U.S. economy contracted 1 percent. For all of 2009, forecasts Barclays Capital, the developing economies of

Asia will have grown 5.2 percent, while the U.S. gross domestic product will have shrunk by 2.3 percent.

Unfortunately, high economic growth does not ensure high stock returns. Incredible as it may sound, *the faster a country's economy grows, the worse an investment its stock market tends to be.* "People have hopelessly got the wrong end of the story," warns Elroy Dimson of the London Business School, who is one of the world's leading authorities on financial markets.*

Based on decades of data from 53 countries, Professor Dimson and his colleagues have found that the economies with the highest growth produce the lowest stock returns. Stocks in countries with the highest economic growth have earned an annual average return of 6 percent; those in the slowest-growing nations have gained an average of 12 percent annually.

That's not a typo. Over the long run, stocks in the world's hottest economies have performed half as well as those in the coldest. When Professor Dimson presented these findings in a guest lecture at a Yale University finance program in the summer of 2009, "a couple of people just about fell off their chairs," he says. "They couldn't believe it."

*Jason Zweig, "Under the 'Emerging' Curtain," *Wall Street Journal*, July 25, 2009, B1.

But, if you think about this puzzle for a few moments, it's no longer very puzzling. In stock markets, as elsewhere in life, value depends on both quality and price. When you buy into emerging markets, you do get better economic growth—but you don't always get in at a better price.

"It's not that China is growing and everybody else thinks it's shrinking," says Professor Dimson. "You're paying a price that reflects the growth that everybody can see."

It doesn't matter how rapidly the emerging markets grow if you pay too high a price to get that growth. At the end of 2008, in the trough of the bear market, emerging-markets stocks traded at a 38 percent discount to U.S. shares, as measured by the ratio of price to earnings. But by the middle of 2009, as both markets bounced back, emerging markets had moved to only a 21 percent discount.

And make no mistake: Emerging markets should be much cheaper than U.S. stocks, because they are far riskier. The U.S. government, whatever its faults, is not in the habit of confiscating entire industries without their shareholders' permission or creating inflation so severe that you need a wheelbarrow full of money to pay for a loaf of bread. Former Russian president Vladimir Putin liked to throw CEOs in jail and seize their companies if they criticized him. The Chinese government shoots people who disagree with its policies and has been known to put corporate officials to death when management decisions go awry. The next company these governments mess with could be your own.

But why do investors persist in paying too much for stocks in emerging markets? "The logical fallacy is the same one investors fell into with Internet stocks a decade ago," says finance professor Jay Ritter of the University of Florida. "Rapid technological change doesn't necessarily mean that the owners of capital will get the benefits. Neither does rapid economic growth."

High growth draws out new companies that absorb capital, bid up the cost of labor, and drive down the prices of goods and services. That's good news for local workers and global consumers, but it is ultimately bad news for investors. When countries grow fast, the economic pie does expand—but it gets cut into thinner and thinner slices as more companies sell their stock to the public for the first time through initial public offerings (IPOs).

Back in 2003, before emerging markets got hot, one solitary IPO in Russia took in just $14 million from investors. But in 2007, dozens of Russian IPOs raised a total of $42 billion, or 3,000 times as much capital. In 2006 alone, more than 130 Chinese companies issued roughly $60 billion in new shares—20 percent more than the total raised by all U.S. firms combined. And in 2008, at least six of the world's 10 largest initial public offerings of stock were in emerging markets. In the first half of 2009, Asia, Latin America, the Mideast, and Africa accounted for 69 percent of the dollar value of all IPOs worldwide.

Future profits in these countries will now be spread more thinly across dozens of more companies owned by multitudes of new investors. That leaves less for you.

The role of emerging markets, says Professor Dimson, "is to provide diversification, not to add to returns." As an enduring part of your portfolio, emerging markets are a great way to hedge against the hazard of keeping all your money at home; when the United States zigs, emerging markets tend to zag. If you invest patiently over time, you have little to worry about.

But there's a big difference between owning and buying. Owning an emerging markets fund permanently makes sense. Buying one when they're hot—plunging in for the first time with both feet—does not.

Having up to 15 percent of your total U.S. and international stock assets in emerging markets is a valid plan. But be sure to look first at the holdings of the international funds you already own; many keep at least 20 percent of their assets in developing markets. If you have, say, 25 percent of your stock money in an international fund that has 20 percent of its assets in emerging markets, then you already have a 5 percent stake in developing countries. Factor that into your calculation of your total exposure.

But whatever you do, don't pile into emerging markets in a buying panic. Like all performance chasing, this latest investing binge is doomed to disappoint the people who don't understand what they are doing. If you have an uncontrollable urge to jump into the developing world, book a vacation to Rio.

Safe Bets

- Don't fall for the bogus argument that emerging markets are a sure bet to earn higher returns than U.S. markets.
- Do put—and keep—a small portion of your money there for diversification.
- Don't chase their returns only when they're hot.

Chapter Fifteen

WACronyms:
Why Initials Are So
Often the Beginning
of the End

~

If You Can't Say It, You
Shouldn't Own It

IT'S TIME FOR AN OVERVIEW of financial engineering and its acronymic output, which ranges all the way from ABS and ARMs; CARDS and DECS; CBOs, CDOs, CDS, CLOs, CMBS, and CMOs; EIAs; ETFs; HLTs; IPOs; LBOs,

MBOs, and BIMBOs; MBS; PERCs; PINEs; PIPEs; REMICs; RIBs; SAMs; SPACs; SPARQS; STRYPES and TANS; ELKs, LYONs, PRIDEs, TIGRs, STEERS, and ZEBRAs; to NINAs, NINJAs, and other nonsense.

No other institution (with the possible exceptions of the government or the military) spews out acronyms as prolifically as Wall Street. I call these Wall Street acronyms "WACronyms," because they tend to sound innocent when, in fact, many of them are full of wacky complications and incomprehensible risks.

While you shouldn't automatically refuse to invest in a WACronym—some ETFs, or exchange-traded funds, may be worthwhile—these catchy abbreviations are always a signal that you should analyze the underlying investment with extreme caution. A WACronym is a sure sign that somebody is trying to sweet-talk you into buying something you might never invest in without the cutesy come-on of the shorthand name.

In peddling WACronyms, Wall Street's marketers are exploiting a quirk of the human mind that psychologists call "fluency," or our tendency to find familiar or easily processed ideas more appealing than unusual, cumbersome ones.

What Maxwell Perkins Knew

How much would you want to read a book entitled *Trimalchio in West Egg*? You're likely to ask yourself three immediate questions: Who's Trimalchio? Where (or what) is West Egg? And who cares? But when the same book is called *The Great Gatsby*, F. Scott Fitzgerald's masterpiece sounds far more appealing. Fortunately, Fitzgerald's editor, Maxwell Perkins, rejected the great author's inept title and replaced it with his own brilliant choice.

How eager would you be to buy a prescription for a drug called 1-[[3-(6,7-dihydro-1-methyl-7-oxo-3-propyl-1*H*pyrazolo[4,3-*d*]pyrimidin-5-yl)-4-ethoxyphenyl]sulfonyl]-4-methylpiperazine citrate? To any nonchemist, that sounds intimidating, scary, perhaps even toxic—like something you might pour into a clogged sink to burn through the gunk that's clogging the pipes. But once the same drug is renamed "Viagra," it seems natural and appealing.

On average, the more often you see or hear something, the less likely it is to be dangerous. (If it were deadly, it would have killed you on the first or second go-round.) Because whatever our ancestors encountered frequently was less likely to be harmful and more likely to be worth approaching, we have evolved to favor the familiar. Anything that reminds us of common things makes us feel comfortable.

So the easier something is to perceive, remember, or pronounce, the safer it will make us feel—regardless of its actual risk or benefit. A name like Viagra, with its hints of life and vigor and waterfalls, sounds fluent and familiar even when we hear it for the first time.

In a classic psychological experiment, people were shown a series of fictitious names of food additives, all with 12 letters. Some, like Magnalroxate, were fairly easy to pronounce; others, like Hnegripitrom, were a cumbersome mouthful. Asked to imagine that they were reading the names as ingredients on food labels, people rated how safe each additive was likely to be. The unpronounceable additives were, on average, rated 29 percent riskier. The psychologists also presented people with the names of amusement park rides. Some were short, catchy, and pronounceable, like Chunta. Other names were hard for most people to say, like Vaiveahtoishi. With no information about the rides other than their names, people rated the unpronounceable rides an average of 44 percent riskier and more likely to make them sick.*

That's why Wall Street peddles "CMOs" instead of *collateralized mortgage obligations*, "HLTs" instead of *highly leveraged transactions*, "SPACs" instead of *special-purpose acquisition companies*, and "SPARQS" instead of *stock participation accreting redemption quarterly pay securities*. In fact, investment bankers put a great deal of energy

---

*Hyunjin Song and Norbert Schwarz, "If It's Difficult to Pronounce, It Must Be Risky," *Psychological Science* 20, no. 2 (2009): 135–138.

and effort into coming up with product names that can somehow be reduced to a catchy WACronym—because Wall Street knows that a fluent name automatically makes investors more comfortable with risks they do not understand.

Collateralized mortgage obligations is an intimidating 11-syllable mouthful that sounds like something a debt-collection agency might try extracting from you while an ex-wrestler named Bruno dislocates your thumbs. A "CMO," in contrast, sounds short, cool, snappy, and familiar: like a fast-food restaurant, a sports statistic, a video game, a type of sneaker, or a new-model car. You would never guess that by late 2008, some CMOs were worth only a tiny fraction of the original prices at which Wall Street foisted them onto sophisticated investors.

Tickers That Click

The same effect extends to stock tickers, the trading symbols that serve as shorthand for identifying which shares you want to trade. Stocks whose tickers are readily pronounceable or evoke positive images (like BUD, CASH, KAR, or LUV) outperform those with clumsy, meaningless tickers like PXG or BZH—at least in the short run. Knowing this, companies eagerly stake their claims to catchy tickers. In August 2006, Harley-Davidson, Inc., the manufacturer of heavyweight motorcycles, announced that it would change its stock ticker from HDI to HOG (motorcyclists have long nicknamed Harleys "hogs"). In its first two days of trading under the memorable new ticker, Harley's stock gained 5 percent.*

The same is true for the full names of stocks. Researchers recently came up with a set of fictitious names for stocks; some were easy to pronounce and recognize, like "Tanley" and "Vander," while others were much less fluent, like "Xagibdan" and "Yoalumnix." In a psychology lab, dozens of people looked at the list of companies and, with no information other than the names, predicted the returns of their stocks over the coming 12 months. The average forecast: Stocks with easy names would go up 4 percent, while those with cumbersome names would go down 4 percent.

In the late 1990s, when the boom in Internet (or dot-com) stocks was in full swing, firms that changed their corporate names to include ".com," ".net," or "Internet" outperformed other technology stocks by a blistering 89 percent over the two months surrounding the name

---

*Alex Head, Gary Smith, and Julia Wilson, "Would a Stock by Any Other Ticker Smell as Sweet?," working paper, Pomona College, www.economics.pomona.edu/GarySmith/Econ190/tickers.pdf; "HOG to Run on Wall Street," press release, Harley-Davidson, Inc., August 10, 2006. During those two days, the Standard & Poor's 500 index, a measure of overall market performance, rose only 2 percent.

change. Even in conservative Switzerland, investors believe that stocks with fluent names like Emmi, Swissfirst, and Comet will earn higher returns than those with clunky monikers like Actelion, Geberit, and Ypsomed.*

It's as Easy as ABC

In the ancient world, people well understood that the act of naming something is a way of asserting power over it. Adam's very first act, after God creates him in the Book of Genesis, is to name each of the animals, thus fulfilling God's wish that man would "have dominion . . . over every living thing that moveth upon the earth."

So it's vital for investors to remember that Wall Street takes control over investments from the start, through the simple act of naming them. By giving an ugly investment a cute little name, Wall Street can fool many people into thinking it's a cute little investment.

Don't be one of those people. Confronted with any investment that's named with a catchy WACronym, you

*Adam L. Alter and Daniel M. Oppenheimer, "Predicting Short-Term Stock Fluctuations by Using Processing Fluency," *Proceedings of the National Academy of Sciences* 103, no. 24 (June 13, 2006): 9369–9372; Michael J. Cooper, Orlin Dimitrov, and P. Raghavendra Rau, "A Rose. com by Any Other Name," *Journal of Finance* 56, no. 6 (December 2001): 2371–2388; Pascal Pensa, "Nomen Est Omen: How Company Names Influence Short- and Long-Run Stock Market Performance," http://ssrn.com/ abstract=924171.

must fight back with your own acronym. Being on your guard is as easy as ABC: Always Be Cautious. Ask what the WACronym stands for. If you can neither pronounce nor understand the abbreviated terms, don't invest in it.

Safe Bet

- Approach any WACronym with caution. Ask what the initials stand for, and if you can't understand the full terms, don't invest.

Sex

*How Men and Women Think
Differently about Money—and
How They Can Work Together
for Better Investing Results*

FESS UP, FELLOWS: The masters of the universe have turned out to be masters of disaster. No matter which aspect of the financial crisis you consider, there's a man behind it.

So it's worth thinking about how things might have turned out if the financial world were female.

First of all, women value safety. Even after controlling for age, income, and marital status, women are more inclined than men to wear seat belts, avoid cigarette smoking, floss and brush their teeth, and get their blood pressure checked. They have also been shown to be about 40 percent less prone than men to run yellow traffic lights—and are much less likely to cause a fatal car crash.

That caution extends to money. On average, female fund managers take less risk than men, stick to their investing styles more consistently, and end up at either the top or the bottom of the performance charts more rarely. Corporations with female chief financial officers are substantially less likely to issue debt and make acquisitions. Compared to companies whose chief executive officer is a man, firms with female CEOs acquire and merge with other companies at prices that are about 70 percent lower—thus taking over businesses more cheaply and presumably enhancing the value of their own shares over time.

In 2001, a survey of financial analysts and investment advisers found that, compared to men, women felt that it was much more important to avoid incurring large losses, falling below a target rate of return, and acting on incomplete information. In short, women are more risk-averse.

By contrast, in the testosterone-poisoned sandbox of the male investor, the most important thing is beating somebody else; the second most important, bragging about it.

The long term is the next guy's problem, and asking for advice is an admission of inferiority. Worrying about risk is for sissies. Leverage is good, since it raises returns . . . while the market goes up.

Is it any wonder the male-dominated world of Wall Street has boomed and busted every few years, like clockwork, for more than two centuries?

Girls Rule, Guys Drool

When I wrote a column for Mother's Day in the *Wall Street Journal* suggesting that women could teach men a thing or two about investing, I received swarms of furious e-mails from male readers who insisted I was wrong—but who offered no evidence to prove their case.

The evidence is clear that women can and should invest as least as well as men. Women tend to be less afflicted than men by overconfidence, or the delusion that they know more than they really do. And they are more likely than men to attribute success to factors outside themselves, like luck or fate.

Women also care less than men about "the adrenaline rush, the play element, the bragging rights" that come from trading competitively, says Vickie Bajtelsmit, chair of the finance department at Colorado State University. While men and women alike believe that their own portfolios will beat the market, surveys have shown that males expect to outperform by a margin one-third wider than females do. On average, women tend to be considerably less competitive than men.

As a result of these differences, women tend to rely more on expert advice, trade less frequently, hold less volatile portfolios, and expect lower returns than men do. In short, they make better investors; finance professors Brad Barber and Terrance Odean have found that women's risk-adjusted returns beat those of men by an average of about one percentage point annually. Professors Barber and Odean measured performance over a generally bullish period; in a time of falling markets, women may outperform men by a wider margin still.

Feelings

"There's a general emotional difference between men and women as they perceive and take risks," says Jennifer Lerner, a psychologist at Harvard University's John F. Kennedy School of Government.

Negative events like natural disasters, terrorist attacks, or financial crises usually make men more angry than fearful. Women, in contrast, tend to feel more fearful than angry.

Those differing emotions lead to divergent viewpoints. Seen through what Professor Lerner calls "a lens of anger," the world seems more certain, more amenable to our control, and less risky. Just think of your physical stance when you are angry: You move forward, approaching whatever or whoever has angered you. Viewed through a lens of fear, however, the world appears full of uncertainty, beyond our control, and rife with risk. When you are fearful, you step back or turn away from the source of your fear.

The results of a nationwide survey of hundreds of investors conducted in March 2009, just days after the Dow Jones Industrial Average bottomed at 6,547, show how anger and fear in the minds of men and women can affect their financial decisions. Women were more than twice as likely as men to say they were "much more fearful than angry" about the financial crisis. And one in eight men, but only one in every 40 women, had "made riskier investments looking for long-term growth" in the previous week. Female investors were twice as likely to expect the return on stocks over the coming year to be zero or negative—and twice as likely to think stocks will return 5 percent or less per year over the decade to come.

"The women were more concerned—and fearful—but took fewer actions than men," says psychologist Ellen Peters of the University of Oregon, who co-directed the survey. "They were also more pessimistic—or realistic?—about what to expect from the market."

Because fear reduces the tendency to take a new course of action, women are more inclined than men to wait out a scary market decline.

More to Lose

It's no wonder women are more realistic and less risk-loving than men; for one thing, they have more to lose. Historically, explains Vickie Bajtelsmit of Colorado State University, women have had:

- Lower average wages.
- Less access to credit.
- More responsibility for taking care of children and parents.
- Less time in the workforce.
- Lower probability of being covered by a defined benefit pension plan.
- Longer life expectancy.

The gap is narrowing, but taking time out of the workforce to have and raise children still deprives the average woman of years of wage increases and retirement-plan contributions; it may also reduce her future Social Security benefits. Women will, on average, have to live longer on less money than men. Since they're perfectly well aware of that, it's only rational for women to respond by being more cautious.

In fact, even when they work as security analysts and investment advisers, women tend to focus much more than men do on ways to reduce the risk of their portfolios; men fixate on how to increase the return. (It's worth pointing out here that raising a portfolio's return is much like inflating a tire. You can pump it up, then pump it up some more, and everything will seem fine as you keep pumping—until the very instant it blows to smithereens.)

The Marriage of Minds

Couples can work better together as investors if they recognize each other's strengths and weaknesses, as well as their own.

Women are more likely than men to look at a larger set of alternatives and to deliberate over many different choices. But once they make a decision, they are more inclined to stick with it. Those characteristics can frustrate men, but they are also a valuable counterweight to the more impetuous style of male decision making. In financial life, there are no prizes for making the *fastest* decision—but there are many rewards for making the *best* decision.

There's some evidence that women have an unusual kind of sensitivity. They seem to be more skeptical about low-risk investments. Female investment professionals rated insured savings accounts as twice as risky as men did, and regarded Treasury bonds as about 25 percent riskier. Since investors often suffer the worst damage on investments that are supposedly the safest, men should make a special point of having their wives review any choices the husbands regard as a sure thing.

The female antenna is more acute in another sense, too. Research suggests that women are more sensitive to nonverbal cues, like gestures and facial expressions, that may betray a lack of trustworthiness.* And women are more likely to spot such "tells" if they step into a conversation that is well underway. At that point the man may already have been caught up in a bond of developing trust, but the woman will bring a more objective outside perspective.

So, if a couple is scheduled to meet with a financial adviser for the first time, the woman should arrive separately, preferably at least five minutes after the meeting has already begun. The man can simply say at the outset, "My wife is running a little late, so she wants us to get started without her." The husband and wife can then compare notes, after the meeting, about their separate first impressions to be sure they are equally comfortable with the adviser.

Because women, especially mothers, are so busy, they may find single-step solutions more appealing. For example,

*See, for example, www.columbia.edu/~dc2534/slices.in.press.page.numbers.oct.2007.pdf.

a life-cycle or lifestyle fund, which balances stocks, bonds, and cash together into a single, simple portfolio that automatically grows more conservative as you age, saves investors the trouble of doing any trading themselves. These funds are not perfect—I generally advise staying away from a life-cycle fund that has more than 80 percent in stocks in its most aggressive years and more than 20 percent in stocks in its most conservative years—but they are usually well-diversified and can provide a strong foundation for the entire household portfolio. If a woman puts much of her money in a life-cycle fund, her holding can counteract many of the dangerous stunts that her husband might pull with his part of the family assets.

When husband and wife (or boyfriend and girlfriend) share the responsibility for investing, they should not let a competition develop. A man may say something like "If you think you're so smart, then let's measure our performance and see who makes more money investing." Don't go there, guys—and women, don't let them. What matters is not whether one of you beats the other. What matters, instead, is whether each of you is getting both of you closer to your common goal of financial security for the family.

Above all, men must recognize that their wives need to take some charge of the family's money. The average woman will outlive her husband by roughly five years—assuming that their divorce or his disability does not force financial independence upon her prematurely. Sooner or later, it is virtually inevitable that the woman will be running the family's money. It is irresponsible for a husband to keep such tight control of the family's investments that his wife will find them completely unfamiliar after he is gone. And it is foolish for a woman not to insist on taking charge of at least a portion of the family's money.

So, men, listen up: Your household's investment portfolio will be better diversified if your spouse or partner helps manage it. She will share in what comes out of that portfolio down the road; shouldn't she share in what goes into it?

The magic words for a man to say are: "I want you to have as much control as you want." Chances are, her ideas and emotions will complement yours, and you will both end up wealthier. At least one of you will end up wiser.

Safe Bets

- Men and women should arrive at different times to interview a financial adviser.
- A husband should have his wife review his "sure thing" investing ideas.
- Spouses should cooperate, not compete, on their investments.

Chapter Seventeen

Mind Control

~

Keeping Your Unconscious Biases from Making Decisions for You

WHEN YOU INVEST, your mind has a mind of its own.

At the very moment when you are most convinced of your own rationality, you may be feeling rather than thinking your way toward a decision. You can often be in the grip of emotions you do not even know you have—leading you to make choices you will later regret.

This chapter will show you some of the remarkable ways your mind runs on autopilot beneath the level of awareness. Your mind is full of anchors and frames, magnets and halos. Psychologists call these mental patterns "unconscious biases," since they can taint your judgments even though you have no awareness of their influence. Your mind has many more quirks than we can possibly cover here; this is just a sampling.*

It's possible that nothing I can tell you will make you believe you are prone to unconscious biases. (If you were aware that you have them, they wouldn't be unconscious biases!) But denying they exist cannot make them go away. Only by instituting the right rules to govern your behavior can you counteract the influence of unconscious biases.

Anchors Aweigh

To see how anchors work, take the last three digits of your cell phone number, then add 400. (If, for instance, your phone number ends in 342, that gives you 742.) Now consider: Did Genghis Khan found the Mongol Empire before or after the year that matches your phone number plus 400? And what's your best guess of the exact year he founded the Mongol Empire?

---

*For more on the frailties of the investing mind, see Gary Belsky and Thomas Gilovich, *Why Smart People Make Big Money Mistakes and How to Correct Them* (New York: Free Press, 2010) and Jason Zweig, *Your Money and Your Brain* (New York: Simon and Schuster, 2007).

Typically, the higher the last three digits of your phone number are, the later the date you will estimate for the founding of the Mongol Empire. (The actual year was 1206.)

That's the power of anchoring. In a world awash with uncertainty, your mind automatically estimates unknown values by anchoring onto the first number that happens to pop into your head. You know that cell phones have nothing to do with medieval marauders, but the digits based on your phone number influence your judgment nevertheless.

No wonder marketers try to control exactly which number does pop into your head. Why do money managers nearly always launch mutual funds with an initial value of exactly $10 per share? Why, when you are looking to buy a house, do real-estate agents usually show you the most expensive place first? Why do Wall Street analysts tend to set perfectly even price targets for a stock, like $50 instead of $48.93 or $51.02?

A $10 share price for a mutual fund is a nice round number, and well below the price for the average stock—making the fund look cheap at the outset. If you look at the most expensive house first, its price will lodge in your memory, making all the other houses you see that day look like bargains by comparison. A $50 price target is a lot easier to hold in mind than $48.93.

Anchors have a magnetic, almost magical effect. When the Dow Jones Industrial Average is at 9,999, you will feel much more certain that the market is about to break 10,000 than you would feel at 9,998 or 9,995. As prices approach the threshold of a round number, their next move can seem almost inevitable.

You must resist the pull of anchors like these. A stock is not cheap or expensive merely because its price is below or above a particular number. It is cheap or expensive only in relation to the fundamental value of the underlying business, which has *nothing* to do with whether the share price is near an anchor. If you find yourself getting excited over any investment based purely on its price, you're anchoring. Pull the hook out of your head and start over, focusing on the value of the business instead.

You've Been Framed

Would you rather eat a hamburger that's 90 percent lean or one that's 10 percent fat? Unless you're a vegetarian, the thought of the first burger probably has you salivating already, while the second lands in your imagination with a greasy splat. Even if you realize that both are two ways of describing the identical piece of meat, you can't get the effect out of your head: These are both the same burger, and yet they are not.

Likewise, how you feel about an investment depends on whether you are faced with its positive or its negative aspects. When your financial planner tells you that you stand a 90 percent chance of hitting your retirement goals if you follow a particular strategy, it will sound like an excellent idea. If he tells you that you stand a 10 percent chance of not having enough money to retire, it will suddenly sound like a very bad idea. And if he tells you that one out of every 10 people who have invested this way came up short of their goals, it will sound like a terrible idea.

Of course, all three are different ways of saying the same thing—but each of them comes with very different emotional baggage. The frame of 90 percent success puts you in mind of the comforts and pleasures you hope to have in retirement. The frame of 10 percent failure reminds you of your worries about not having enough money to live on. And the description of the one in 10 people who came up short will ignite all your most personal fears of failure. That "one person" is you!

The way to control framing is by *reframing*. Whenever a marketer or financial salesperson is pitching anything to you, turn the numbers inside out. When someone talks about a 90 percent chance of success, you should automatically ask yourself whether you are comfortable with 10 percent odds of failure. If someone says you could double your money if you are right, ask how much you could lose if you are wrong.

Then be sure to consider the impact of those potential gains or losses not just on the value of that one holding, but on your entire portfolio—shifting from the narrow frame of one investment viewed in isolation to the broader frame of all your investments taken as a whole.

You can also reframe not just in space, but in time. A 20 percent drop in your portfolio since the beginning of the year can be terrifying. But don't forget to look at how the value of your account has changed over your entire holding period. You may actually be sitting on a sizable profit over the long run despite the painful losses you've incurred in the short run. Looking at your returns through the frames of several time periods—say, the past three years, the past five years, and ever since you opened the account—is the best way to tell.

Magnets in Your Mind

In the 1960s, a psychologist named Robert Zajonc (pronounced ZYE-ontz) ran an extraordinary series of experiments. He flashed images before people's eyes for the tiniest fraction of a second. Was it a face, a photograph of a car, a drawing of a frog, a word? No one could say: At best, most viewers said that all they could discern was a flash of light.

Later, Professor Zajonc showed the same people a set of images. Most they had never seen before. But some were among those they had been exposed to, for a few thousandths of a second, in his laboratory. It turned out they liked those images much better than the others, even though they had no idea they had ever seen them before and had, in fact, been exposed to them for as little as one-thousandth of a second, or 300 times faster than the blink of an eye.

Professor Zajonc named this phenomenon "mere exposure." Simply having been in the presence of something, regardless of whether you ever were aware of it, makes you like it better. Familiarity acts as a kind of magnet in your mind, making you feel closer to whatever you have encountered before—regardless of its merit.

The investing mind is full of these magnets.

U.S. investors, for example, keep an average of more than 80 percent of their stock money invested in American companies, even though the United States accounts for less than 50 percent of the value of all the planet's stock markets. On average, American investors could double the proportion of international stocks they hold and still be underinvested overseas. The whole world is similarly xenophobic; investors in most countries tend to over-weight the stocks from their own markets. Investors everywhere would be better off owning more in markets that are less familiar to them.

Chances are, you also are more comfortable investing in companies whose products, logos, and advertising jingles are familiar to you—Coca-Cola, Nike, Sony, Apple

Computer. In fact, you should be skeptical; there's evidence that the stocks of familiar companies can get bid up to unsustainably high prices, leading to disappointing future returns.

So, whenever an investing strategy feels familiar to you or seems obvious, try making it unfamiliar. If you have all your stock money in U.S. companies, ask yourself whether you would want to do so if you were Chinese or Senegalese. What would attract you about American stocks in that case, and what risks might you worry about? If Coca-Cola is your favorite stock, imagine for a moment that you had never tasted a Coke. What would you then want to know about the business prospects of the Coca-Cola Company in order to find it an attractive investment?

What Springs to Mind

If we were all strictly logical, we would judge how frequent or likely something is by how often it has occurred in the past.

We are not all strictly logical.

Instead of judging how probable something is, instead we judge how vivid and memorable it is. That's why people bite their nails at the very thought of flying in a plane—and may even light up a cigarette or have another double Scotch to calm themselves down. Airplane crashes are extremely rare, but when they do happen they are broadcast online and on TV until the fireball, the smoking wreckage, the cries of the families are inescapable. Cigarettes and Scotch kill vastly more people than airplanes do, but they kill one person at a time in slow motion, destroying a few body cells with each puff or sip, rather than dozens of people at once in a few seconds of fiery terror.

The more vivid and dreadful a risk seems, the more uncontrollable and sudden or unpredictable it appears, the more likely it will feel to happen. Thus, we think death by shark attack or lightning strike is far more common than it really is; we are more afraid of cancer, which is largely outside our control, than we are of heart disease, which is partly within our control. And investors think constantly, almost obsessively, about avoiding another market crash. But they give very little thought to insuring against inflation—which does its destructive work not suddenly and dreadfully, but in dribs and drabs over the course of decades.

So, when you think about risks, first ask whether you are worrying about the right thing. There may be a more subtle—but much more dangerous—risk that you have overlooked. And don't just size up the probabilities and rewards of being right. Be sure you also make an honest effort to evaluate the consequences of being wrong.

The Halo Effect

Rating one aspect of someone's personality changes how you assess everything else about the person. For instance, once you were asked to grade how handsome I am, your answer would then influence your rating of my intelligence, my athletic ability, my effectiveness as a leader, and so on. Say you gave me a perfect "10" for looks; that, in turn, would automatically raise your estimates of how smart and athletic I am.*

This is known as the halo effect, since the rating of one quality throws a kind of halo over any other quality that is evaluated later. It happens to investors all the time. A rising stock price makes a CEO look smarter. A successful product launch makes the bosses look like geniuses. A financial adviser in a suit and tie probably will seem a lot more trustworthy than one in a T-shirt and torn jeans.

But, of course, none of those things are really true. A CEO does not become smarter when the company's stock price goes up (in fact, the CEO may become dumber, as a rising stock may lead him or her to take reckless risks). A new product may have been the result of luck, not design. And the quality of advice is not contingent on the adviser's clothes.

*It would also show that you need to get your eyes checked, but that's a different story.

To combat the halo effect, evaluate the investment just by the numbers. Include it as one in a set of similar companies or funds. Delete all names and references that could help you tell which is which. Then analyze all the different choices on a purely numerical basis and pick the best. (Try getting someone else to help you by censoring or redacting all the details that could betray the identity of what you are appraising.) With only the raw numbers to go on, you become less prone to any halo effects cast by the CEO, the company's products, or other influences that might make it impossible for you to be objective.

The Prediction Addiction

One of the wonders of the human brain is our ability to recognize patterns in the world around us, often without any conscious awareness of how we do it. A centerfielder may start moving toward where the ball is likely to go before the batter even hits it. An ambulance worker may recognize the signs of a heart attack before any monitoring equipment can confirm it. A grandmaster chess player can tell, with a split-second glance at the board, how many moves it should take to win the game.

But this power, so often a blessing, can also be a curse. In environments like baseball, an ambulance, or a chess tournament, feedback is prompt and unambiguous: Either running toward shallow right field was the right thing to do or it was a mistake. Nor does the centerfielder have to wait days, weeks, months, or years to find out.

In the financial world, however, feedback is delayed, incomplete, and ambiguous. You buy a stock at 10. A few seconds later, it falls to 9: You are wrong. Moments after that, it is at 10.50: Now you are right. A week later, it is at 6: Now you are wrong. Then word comes that Warren Buffett, the world's leading investor, is buying it: Now you are right. Two weeks after you bought it, the stock is at 15, so you sell it to lock in a 50 percent profit. Six months later, however, it is at 40: Now you were wrong to sell.

Thus, in the stock market, much of what seems to be patterns is, in fact, just random noise, like drops of food coloring unfurling into intricate clouds in a glass of water. If you think you can predict the next particular swirl, your eyes are playing tricks on you; it cannot be done.

But the feeling is there, all the same. Investors who make money a few trades in a row become convinced that they can predict the next twitch in the market. Like a basketball player whose every shot seems predestined to swish through the heart of the net, they have a hot hand; they are on a roll. Investors and traders rely on countless tools that purport to be able to capture whatever the market is about to do.

And the human mind jumps to conclusions about long-term trends from very short-term samples. Neuroscientists have shown that it takes only two repetitions of anything for your brain to conclude that a third repetition is more than likely. That's why so many people say, "This stock is going up," when, in truth, all we can be sure of is "This stock has been going up." A stock that has gone up two trades in a row is not more likely to go up on the third, any more than a coin that has come up heads twice in a row is bound to come up heads again on the next toss.

This automatic tendency to forecast the unpredictable is what I call the "prediction addiction." You can best fight it by tracking all your forecasts: Every time you get that uncanny feeling that you know what the markets will do, write it down, including your specific predictions of what will happen and when. If you make an honest effort to build a complete record of your forecasts, you will learn one of two things: Either you are good enough at forecasting to become a professional, or you should stop bothering to try.

The Blind Spot in Your Brain

Finally, it's time to discuss the most dangerous bias of all: your belief that you are unbiased. Research by Emily Pronin, a psychologist at Princeton University, has shown that people are quite accurate at identifying potential sources of bias in other people's judgments—but very poor at seeing the same biases in their own. Professor Pronin calls this the "bias blind spot."

Think of it this way: Have you ever had a really bad day and then taken out your frustration by screaming at a waiter, a checkout clerk, or your spouse or children? After you have calmed down, what do you tell yourself? Chances are it's not *Wow, I am really a rude person*, but rather something more like *Wow, I really lost my temper*. Now, however, imagine that you are a witness to a man screaming at a waiter, a checkout clerk, or his family members. Which conclusion are you more likely to come to now: *Wow, that guy really lost his temper* or *Wow, that guy is really a rude person*?

You will almost certainly conclude that you lost your temper, while the other person was rude. What is very unlikely to occur to you is that the other person, observing both himself and you, would come to the opposite conclusion: I lost my temper, but *you* were rude!

When thinking about yourself, you naturally focus on what distinguishes this particular situation from the normal circumstances you find yourself in. When thinking about someone else, however, you know nothing about that individual's particular circumstances. So, instead of basing your judgment on the uniqueness of his temporary *situation*, you leap to conclusions about his permanent *disposition*. Meanwhile, the other person does the same about you. Each of you is blind to your own bias.

In much the same way, we can recognize that other people's judgments might be tainted by anchoring or framing, by familiarity or vividness, by the halo effect or the prediction addiction—but we refuse to believe that these biases affect our own thinking. In other words, you think it is silly for the average person to believe that he or she is above average—and yet you remain convinced that *you* are above average!

The ultimate lesson is simple: None of us is perfectly rational. We all make mental mistakes. The only way to rise above them, and to start to minimize them, is by recognizing our own human frailty. It is much harder to know yourself, truly and deeply, than you may ever have imagined.

Safe Bets

- Fight anchoring by asking what a stock should be worth, not what its current price is.
- Reframe by inverting data.
- Try to make information unfamiliar by analyzing it as if you were a stranger to the facts.
- Track your forecasts.
- Remember that you are prone to the same biases you recognize in others.

Chapter Eighteen

Financial Planning Fakery

~

What Is Your Risk Tolerance?
No One Knows!

It's conventional wisdom among financial planners that every investor has a distinctive appetite for risk. Most financial advisers will subject you to a risk-tolerance questionnaire, a series of between a half-dozen and a hundred questions supposedly designed to determine whether you are a spineless wimp or a wild-eyed thrill seeker.

If you are perceptive, you will notice three peculiar things about these questionnaires.

The first is that many of the questions have nothing to do with investing. You might, for example, be asked: *If your flight is scheduled to leave at 7 P.M., what time would you choose to arrive at the airport?* or *When the posted speed limit is 55 mph, how fast do you prefer to drive?* I haven't yet found a question asking whether at 3:25 in the morning you would rather eat chicken, oysters, broccoli, or bananas, but I've only seen a few dozen of these questionnaires. There's probably one like that out there somewhere.

The second oddity about these questionnaires is that many feature the sort of trivia challenges you might face on a Wall Street version of *Jeopardy: From 1926 through 2008, the average annual return on stocks was: (a) 11.7 percent, (b) 2.9 percent, (c) 9.4 percent, (d) 5.6 percent* or *The bond that has the longest duration, or sensitivity to changes in interest rates, is: (a) a 20-year municipal bond, (b) a 20-year investment-grade corporate bond, (c) a 20-year zero-coupon Treasury bond, (d) a 20-year Treasury Inflation-Protected Security.* Any fifth grader could immediately see that what these questions test is not your tolerance of risk, but your knowledge of investing. If you get a high score, you are a master of Wall Street minutiae. But that doesn't mean you have a high tolerance for taking financial risk; it means only that you could go to a cocktail party and bore everyone to death.

The third flaw in these quizzes is that some of the questions simply make no sense: *If the stock market fell 20 percent, you would: (a) buy, (b) sell, (c) do nothing.* But if you knew the answer to that kind of question, then you would already understand your own risk tolerance! And in that case, there would be no point in sitting through such a cockamamie quiz.

The Dimensions of Risk

In fact, "risk tolerance" is a myth. No one has a fixed attitude toward investing risk. Your willingness to take chances with your money will vary:

- *Over time.*

    When the economy is strong and markets are rising, you will take extra risk. When recession and a bear market hit, suddenly you won't want to take any unnecessary risk. You are the same person, but your risk tolerance is very different at those two times.

- *Across space.*

    You buy lottery tickets every once in a while; you may even enjoy an annual visit to a casino. But you also insist on carrying life insurance, home insurance, disability insurance, and health insurance. Is your risk tolerance high or low? It's both: You are risk-seeking in one area of your financial life and risk-averse in another.

- *By physical state.*

     If a woman pats you softly on the shoulder, you will become considerably more willing to take financial risk.* And looking at sexy photographs can temporarily turn the meekest investors into aggressive risk seekers. However, being moderately hungry will make you much less willing to part with your money.

- *Depending on how you earned the money.*

     Imagine getting $10,000. Chances are you would take a lot of risk with it if you won it playing Lotto. If you got the same $10,000 as a year-end bonus, you would take less risk. If you inherited it from your grandmother, you might take no risk at all.

- *According to how the investment is described.*

     As we saw in Chapter 17, how an investment is framed will make a huge difference in how risky it seems to you. You will invest in a strategy with a 90 percent success rate, but you would turn it down if you heard it had a 10 percent chance of failing. Same investment, different description: varying risk tolerance.

- *Based on recent gains and losses.*

     If your last few trades have been profitable, you may believe you are on a roll, inducing you to

---

*Even if you are female.

take risks you would never assume if your results were neutral or negative. You might also take extra risk when your recent investments have fared badly, just as a racetrack gambler who's down for the day may bet all his money on the last race in a desperate ploy to get back into the black. In other words, the next risk you take may depend on how the last few happened to work out.

- *By social setting.*

    In the privacy of your home, you might be a very conservative investor. But if you go to a barbecue at a friend's house and get stuck listening to the neighborhood braggart boasting about how much money he made trading leveraged exchange-traded funds (ETFs), the next thing you know you may end up buying some of the things yourself. Like a group of teenagers playing chicken with their cars, investors can do things under social pressure that they would never do in isolation.

Thus there are at least seven factors that can change your tolerance for risk from moment to moment. An extremely aggressive investor can be made into a wimp by a few subtle changes to the environment, while a couple of tweaks here and there can turn even a scaredy-cat into a risk-seeking tiger.

That's why one of my favorite investing rules is "If the market is open, your wallet should be closed." You should never act on an investing idea the same day you get it; the next day, your mood and situation will have changed, and the facts may look different to you. Sleeping on it is one of the simplest and best ways to make sure your decision is not just a momentary whim.

So don't bother wasting your time taking a meaningless risk-tolerance test. Your tolerance for taking risk is so changeable there's no point trying to measure it.

What does matter, however, is your *capacity* for taking risk. And that cannot be measured with a cutesy questionnaire. Instead, it requires a detailed analysis of your present and future financial situation. How much money do you have? How much can you afford to lose? How might your future needs for income and spending change? How far along are you in the effort to reach your financial goals?

A good financial planner can give you expert guidance in answering these questions and finding solutions to any problems that the questions expose. But first you have to find the right person to provide you with that advice.

Safe Bet

- Sleep on it. If the market is open, your wallet should be closed. Always wait until the next day to act, in order to see whether the facts still seem the same.

Chapter Nineteen

Advice on Advice

~

How to Find a Good
Financial Adviser

IN A PERFECT WORLD, STOCKBROKERS and financial planners
would work patiently with you to understand your needs and
your goals. They would carefully craft a financial plan cover-
ing every aspect of your life, then write an investment policy
statement to guide all your portfolio decisions. They would
counsel you on how to minimize your debts and expenses
and how to maximize your assets and income. When markets plunge, they would calm you with words of encourage-
ment; when markets soar, they would sober you with words

of warning. They would cut your taxes to the bone; they would almost never make any trades, buying only whatever has gone down in price and selling only when you need the cash or a tax break. In a perfect world, financial advisers would be to all aspects of your money what your minister, priest, or rabbi is to your soul: a wise counsel and steward who puts your best interests ahead of their own.

The world isn't perfect.

All too many brokers and planners regard themselves as producers whose job is to wring as much fee revenue out of you as they can. Just as you'd be lucky to get 30 minutes out of your doctor for your annual physical, you may have a hard time getting any sustained attention out of your financial adviser. And there's plenty of evidence that, instead of helping you buy low and sell high, many advisers may be even more inclined to buy high and sell low than you are yourself.

But you can make a good match, and a good adviser can be worth at least his or her weight in gold. This chapter will give advice on how to get advice, how to tell whether it's good, and how to benefit from it.

Why Bother?

Do you need advice?

The mere fact that you are reading this book suggests that you might. To be honest, almost everyone can benefit from good financial advice. The heads of Wall Street's biggest firms, the CEOs of mutual fund companies, and many financial advisers themselves all have someone help them with their investment, retirement, tax, and estate issues.

And no wonder. In the United States, you can easily run afoul of the hundreds of highly technical laws and regulations that mandate how to invest, manage, exchange, withdraw, bequeath, account for, and pay taxes on your money. Various accounts are overseen by the U.S. Department of Labor, the Internal Revenue Service, the Securities and Exchange Commission, state regulators, and even local courts. In 2005, the U.S. tax code and regulations already contained 9.1 million words.*

Mistakes can be costly. The tax authorities can audit you and penalize you if they find what they claim to be errors; overlooking rules and requirements can disqualify you from being eligible for tax deductions; clerical oversights can cost thousands of dollars to correct.

Finally, getting advice also offers an important psychological benefit. If a decision turns out to be right, you can pat yourself on the back for having chosen a good adviser. But if it turns out to be wrong, you can blame the adviser instead of kicking yourself. Having someone else to blame can prevent

*www.taxfoundation.org/research/show/1961.html.

you from giving up on your financial plan when the results are discouraging.

Finding Advice

Begin your search inside yourself. What kind of advice do you need? Not all so-called financial planners provide a broad range of services; many do little more than plunk their clients into a portfolio of mutual funds and exchange-traded funds and then charge 1 percent a year in perpetuity for keeping them there. If all you want is someone to tell you where to put how much of your money, this kind of financial planning may be fine. But if, as is more likely, you want someone who can advise you on when to take distributions from a retirement account or how to calculate the taxable gain on futures contract, then you need more than a mere fund picker.

Any financial planner, financial adviser, or wealth manager worthy of the name should always:

- Voluntarily disclose all fees and commissions as well as any potential conflicts of interest that might influence any recommendations to you.
- Prepare a comprehensive financial plan that (among other things) itemizes your family budget, lists your current assets and liabilities, and projects your future spending needs.

- Develop an investment policy statement (IPS), summarizing your investing objectives, your need for liquidity, your tax situation, the level of risk you are willing to assume, the time horizon over which the money will be invested, the kinds of assets that are appropriate for your money, and any special limitations you may have (for example, an unwillingness to own tobacco stocks).
- Periodically review with you, in person, your progress toward meeting the goals outlined in your financial plan and how well your accounts are complying with the standards set out in your IPS.

Start by visiting www.napfa.org to identify financial planners who charge only fees, not commissions, and http://pfp.aicpa.org to find certified public accountants who are also qualified to provide financial advice.

Meanwhile, you should also ask the professionals you know best and trust the most—your lawyer, for example, or even your boss—if they can refer you to someone they trust. Ask your friends what they like or dislike about their financial advisers and what mistakes they or their advisers made that you should try to avoid.

When you have your list narrowed down to a handful of candidates, conduct a background check. Ask advisers for a copy of their (or their firms') Form ADV, a document that most money managers overseeing at least $25 million must file with the Securities and Exchange Commission. Check carefully to see whether the adviser or firm has ever been disciplined for improper business conduct and whether the fees you have been quoted are consistent with what other clients have been offered. Because crooked advisers are not above removing a few incriminating pages from the copies of the ADV that they hand out, it's a good idea to obtain your own copy of the form to make sure nothing is missing (try www.adviserinfo.sec.gov). Visit www.finra.org/brokercheck, www.cfp.net/search, and www.nasaa.org to cross-check the disciplinary history.

What to Ask

You should now have two or three candidates left. Make an appointment to meet with each in person. Here are a few questions you should ask:

- What made you want to become a financial adviser?
- Do you focus primarily or exclusively on asset management, or do you also have expertise in taxes, retirement, and estate planning, as well as budgeting and debt management? What education, training, experience, and licenses do you have in these practice areas?

- What is your philosophy of investing? Do you rely mainly on index funds? (If the answer is "No," ask to see evidence that the alternatives actually have worked.) How often do you typically trade for clients?

- How high an average annual return on my investments do you think is feasible? (Anything above 10 percent suggests the adviser is either delusional or dishonest; answers below 8 percent start to make sense.)

- How do you manage risk?

- What needs and goals does your typical client have?

- How many clients do you have, and will you personally manage my account? How much time should I reasonably expect you to devote to me over the course of a typical year?

- Describe something you achieved for a client that makes you proud.

- What's the worst mistake you've made with a client?

- How do you go about resolving conflicts with clients?

- Describe the process you have in mind for helping me achieve my goals. How will you monitor our progress?

- When recommending investments, do you accept any form of compensation from any third party? Why or why not?

- How long will I have to decide whether to commit to actions you recommend? Are there circumstances under which I would have to make my mind up immediately? (That would be a no-no.)

- What are your services likely to cost me in a typical year? What percentage of my assets will you charge in annual fees? How do you report your fees and commissions?

- May I see a sample account statement, and can you explain it to me clearly?

- What does money mean to you? Do you consider yourself financially successful?

- Can you provide me with your resume, both parts of your Form ADV, and at least three references?

- Has a client ever filed a complaint against you? Why did the most recent client who left your firm decide to do so?

As you ask these questions, take written notes not just on how the adviser seems to respond to your queries but also on how the answers make you feel. Do you sense that this person is trustworthy? You should come away feeling that you would have no worries in sharing a close secret with this person—because, sooner or later, you probably will. If you have any doubts, find another adviser.*

What about Me?

Finally, remember that good financial advisers are in high demand. No matter how much you might want to hire them, they might not want you as a client unless you see eye to eye with them. So you should be prepared to answer questions like these:

- Why do you think you need a financial adviser?
- How knowledgeable are you about investing and financial matters, and how confident are you in your knowledge?
- What does money mean to you?
- What are your biggest fears? What are your fondest hopes?
- How much time and energy are you willing to invest in any financial plan we develop?
- What would it take for you to feel our working relationship is successful?
- When someone presents you with evidence that your opinions may be mistaken, how do you respond?

*For a more comprehensive set of questions, see Chapter 10 in Benjamin Graham, *The Intelligent Investor*, updated with new commentary by Jason Zweig (New York: HarperCollins, 2003).

- How do you deal with conflicts or disputes?
- How did you handle your investments during the severe bear market that began in the fall of 2007? With perfect hindsight, what would you have done differently? How has your attitude toward risk changed?

At the end of this process, you should have made a match that makes you feel very comfortable. You should be able to tell your adviser just about anything relevant to your financial life without hesitation. And he or she should be able to be blunt with you, too. That may include telling you things you may not want to hear—that you need to save more, spend less, or even lower your expectations. Just like a romantic relationship, a financial relationship will endure only if it is founded on mutual trust.

Safe Bet

- Invest plenty of time in picking a good financial adviser. It will be one of the most important relationships you ever have, so you want to make just the right match.

Chapter Twenty

Fraudian Psychology

~

*How to Keep Crooks from Getting
Their Mitts on Your Money*

EVERY YEAR, SHYSTERS SEPARATE thousands of innocent
investors from their money. All these con games have a few
features in common: They hype past "success," they churn
up dreams of getting rich quick, they rely on winning your
trust, they reel you in a little bit at a time, and they steadily
push you from safe and familiar choices into risky specula-
tions that you normally would never give houseroom to.
Often, but not always, they play on lifestyle envy, tantalizing

you with visions of living a life as luxurious as that of the con man himself.

Many sophisticated investors believe that scam artists and swindlers prey exclusively on the unsophisticated. They have the luxury of believing this only because no one has tried swindling them—yet.

I'm OK If You're OK

One of the secrets of an effective scam is what's called "social proof."

Imagine that you are walking through a shopping mall when you overhear a passerby saying that she met someone who says he can turn $100 into $1 million in less than a year. You would probably dismiss her as hopelessly naive, even foolish. If, however, your best friend told you the same thing, you would be less inclined to ridicule the idea. And if three of your close friends all told you independently that they had met the same fellow and believe that he's for real, your skepticism would probably change to curiosity.

That's social proof at work. A few hundred years ago, we all would have believed that the world was flat— after all, everyone else did, too.

The main problem with social proof is that it kills your own inclination to ask for independent proof. That's true not just for ordinary people but for the world's leading financial experts as well. In 1995, the Foundation for New

Era Philanthropy, run by a charismatic, white-haired gentleman named John G. Bennett Jr., collapsed after scamming more than $135 million out of churches, universities, a variety of charities, and an honor roll of the most eminent figures in American finance. Among the victims were John M. Templeton Jr., son of the leading mutual-fund manager; philanthropist Laurance Rockefeller; the renowned hedge-fund maven Julian Robertson; William E. Simon, former U.S. secretary of the Treasury; and John C. Whitehead, the former chairman of Goldman Sachs.

Bennett played on his victims' philanthropic motives. He told them that anonymous donors would double any dollars given to his New Era foundation. New Era would then turn around and match, dollar for dollar, any money raised by the charities of his donors' choice.

Bennett maintained a dignified, mysterious silence when asked who the anonymous donors were—leading his millionaire victims to trust him all the more, since he appeared to be a man of such discretion.

Everyone on Bennett's roster of donors took comfort from the participation of the others. To discourage prying eyes, Bennett would not accept any donor who was not nominated directly by one of his existing victims. Honored to be welcomed into the inner circle, not one of them bothered to ask where the money really came from, why the foundation's tax returns showed only a few thousand dollars in interest income on millions of dollars' worth of supposed assets, or why New Era was not even registered as a charitable organization with the office of the attorney general as Pennsylvania state law required. In truth, when a millionaire gave money, Bennett doubled the amount and disbursed it to the donor's favorite charities—as soon as the next check from one of the millionaire's friends cleared.

The lesson: No matter who has already signed on, there is no substitute for doing your own homework. An investment doesn't just have to make sense to other people; it has to make sense to *you*.

New and Improved

Another common sign of a scam is the repackaging of a standard, almost boring, investment into something that sounds innovative and exciting.

In early 2009, the Stanford Group, which had sold at least $8 billion worth of what it called "certificates of deposit (CDs)," collapsed. Stanford's CDs yielded more than 7 percent at a time when market rates ran around 3 percent.

Stanford insisted that what it called CDs were invested in liquid securities, with underlying returns of up to 16 percent "anchored in time-proven conservative criteria," and closely monitored by regulators in the Caribbean island of Antigua.

But certificates of deposit are not normally invested in other securities; they typically represent a bank's promise to pay a stated rate of interest and to repay your principal, and they are guaranteed by the Federal Deposit Insurance Corporation (FDIC).

When something as boring as a CD is suddenly made to yield more than twice the industry average, using an unprecedented technique made possible only by the legal eagles in an offshore tax haven, investors should be more than cautious. They should be afraid.

The Stanford "CDs" were, of course, an extreme manifestation of Wall Street's obsession with selling the mirage of high yield and low risk. Investors are especially vulnerable to such a pitch when interest rates are falling. But any investment that claims to be conventional and yet is quality-controlled by regulators in an obscure foreign country does not make sense.

In fact, the returns on Stanford's so-called CDs seem to have been fabricated, and the proceeds appear to have gone into the pocket of founder R. Allen Stanford to fund his yachting and his obsession with the game of cricket. Of the billions that investors sank into Stanford, most will probably never be recovered.*

---

*www.sec.gov/litigation/litreleases/2009/lr20901-memo.pdf;   www.sec.gov/litigation/ complaints/2009/stanford-first-amended-022709.pdf.

Words to Watch Out For

Hucksters and frauds tend to have a standard vocabulary, densely salted with words that will get your blood racing.

Here are some words and phrases that shysters are fond of and that financially legitimate people are very unlikely to use:

Secret.

Can't lose.

Earn $XXXX per week.

Free money.

I'm on your side.

Limited-time offer.

Offshore.

I would never lie to you.

Confidential proposal.

Guaranteed.

What are you afraid of?

Request for business relationship.

The opportunity of a lifetime.

I need some account information.

Double your money.

A sure thing.

You'll be sorry if you don't.

You have to hurry.

Don't you want to be rich?

Trust me.

Monthly returns.

I can make you a millionaire.

Transfer money.

You can't afford not to own it.

There's no downside.

Prime bank.

Low risk, high return.

The upside is huge.

I need you to commit to this opportunity right now.

Words like these do not necessarily guarantee that you are dealing with someone dishonest. But they are a sure sign that you should be very suspicious and proceed with extreme caution.

The Rush to Get Rich

One of the surest tip-offs that an investment is a scam is a high promised rate of return. Warren Buffett, universally acclaimed as the world's best investor, has generated an average annual return of slightly better than 20 percent over the course of his long career. So why would you believe that someone you've never even heard of can make money grow at rates of 60 percent to 100 percent per year?

A common trick among scam artists is to market their returns on a monthly basis. A 5 percent monthly return sounds both reasonable and feasible; it's comfortingly close to the rates on CDs or mortgages that you are so familiar with. Of course, those other rates are annual, not monthly. Only if you take the trouble to multiply the claimed 5 percent monthly rate by 12 will you notice that it equates to at least a 60 percent annual rate of return.*

A common trick is to couple what sounds like a familiar monthly rate of return with a relatively unfamiliar investing strategy—trading in foreign currencies, commodity futures, stock options, and so on. It's all too easy for you to conclude that even though you don't know anything about the investing strategy, the promised rate of return sounds low enough to be reasonable. You would be

*A 5 percent monthly return is a 60 percent simple annual return and a 79.6 percent annual return when compounded monthly.

far more suspicious if the con artist promised a high rate of return from something unfamiliar.

The other prevalent technique for turning you into a sucker is what many con artists call "flash the cash." You may pick up the phone and hear a voice say, "I'm holding a check here for you in the amount of $574,000," or "We just conducted a drawing, and you have won our Grand Prize of one million dollars!" Even if you are not a greedy person, the very thought of a pile of money with your name on it can be enough to get you to drop your guard. The caller will then ask a variety of personal questions to probe for your vulnerabilities, offering sympathy for your loneliness or other problems. The next thing you know, the caller will seem like a trusted friend—who will then ask you to provide your bank account information or even to send a token sum of money, say a few thousand dollars, in order to facilitate the transfer of the jackpot to you.

How to Stay Safe

Two good sources of further information on how to armor yourself against being victimized by a fraud are the National Association of Securities Dealers (NASD) Investor Fraud Study Final Report (available at www.sec.gov/news/press/extra/seniors/nasdfraudstudy051206.pdf) and the book *Weapons of Fraud* by Anthony Pratkanis and Doug Shadel (AARP, 2006). If you have aging parents, you should recognize that the elderly are the primary targets of fraud; get mom and dad to be on their guard before it is too late.

Here are a few rules for keeping con artists from stealing your money:

- Never open any e-mail from anyone who claims to be offering lottery tickets, high investing returns, a stake in someone else's inheritance, or sweepstakes winnings. Anyone who has the genuine ability to make you rich would not be telling you about it in an e-mail. Be ruthless and thorough in moving unsolicited financial e-mails into your spam folder.

- Never provide bank account or any other financial information—including your address, date of birth, Social Security number, and so on—to a stranger.

- Never give or send money, by any means, to anyone you do not know.

- Never invest in anything on the recommendation of a friend or family member alone. Always use the kind of checklist featured in Chapter 12 to filter every opportunity that comes your way. Never make any investment the same day you hear about it; always sleep on it and take the time to research it thoroughly.

- Anyone touting a monthly rate of return is highly likely to be a shyster.

- Remember that the expression "If it sounds too good to be true, it probably is" is not quite accurate. If it sounds too good to be true, it *definitely* is. Getting rich quick isn't just difficult or a secret art; it's an impossibility. Anyone who tells you otherwise is a fraud.

Safe Bets

- Beware of letting a telephone conversation continue merely because the person on the other end sounds nice or claims to be able to make you rich. Feel free to ask, "Is this a solicitation?" or to say, "I never invest in anything without doing my own homework first."

- Tell the caller that you will consider investing only if the offer is made in writing. There's no conceivable reason why a legitimate person offering a valid investment shouldn't be willing to provide you with a written description that discloses the relevant facts and risks. If the caller declines to do that, it is a scam.

- Feel free to end the call at any time simply, briefly, and politely: "I'm very sorry, but I'm really not interested. Please place me on your do-not-call list. Thank you. Good-bye."

- Hang up.

Chapter Twenty-One

The Terrible Tale of the Missing $10 Trillion

~

Why Investments Earn Higher Returns Than the Investors Who Own Them

In 1982, THE TOTAL VALUE of the U.S. stock market, as measured by the Dow Jones Wilshire 5000 index, was $1.2 trillion. By late 2007, stocks had grown at an average annual rate of 13.3 percent—enough to turn that $1.2 trillion into $28.2 trillion. Yet the total market value of U.S.

stocks ended up at $18.7 trillion. Nearly $10 trillion was missing. Where did it go?

From the beginning of 1998 through the end of 2001, Kinetics Internet fund generated an average annual return of 42.4 percent—one of the most scorching hot streaks ever achieved by a mutual fund. Yet the average investor in the fund *lost* 15.8 percent annually over that period, trailing the performance of the fund itself by an astonishing 58.2 percentage points per year. Where did people go wrong?

How can investors possibly earn less than their own investments?

This chapter will chronicle the central tragedy of investing behavior and help you understand how to avoid it yourself.

Buy and Hold—Or Buy High and Fold?

Investments don't make or lose money. Investors do.

Investment returns are hypothetical, not real. They are calculated as if everyone bought at the beginning, stayed put, reinvested all dividends and capital gains, and sold only at the end. But investors do not buy low and sell high. They do not even buy and hold. Instead, they buy high and fold—getting in at the top, then bailing out at the bottom.

If you think you have a high tolerance for risk but all you really have is a high tolerance for making money, you will sell in a panic whenever your investments go down. Or, at the very least, you will refuse to add more money at the exact moment when it is most advantageous: after a market crash has declared a clearance sale on stocks. Either way—bailing out at the bottom or declining to buy more when the merchandise is at its cheapest—you end up lowering your ultimate return.

As the market commentator George J.W. Goodman ("Adam Smith") once said, if you don't know who you are, the stock market is a very expensive place to find out.

If you chronically buy *after* performance has been great, and sell (or freeze) *before* performance recovers, your own results will stink. Meanwhile, measured over the entire period of good and bad performance taken together, the returns of the fund or stock may look great. The investment may have done well, even though you as an investor did not.

Thus, the returns reported in the newspaper and on financial web sites are barely better than imaginary. They state how you would have done if you had acted the way most investors are incapable of acting: buying on day one and then hanging on for dear life.

Just how unrealistic are the commonly reported results?

- A study of U.S. mutual funds from 1991 through 2004 found that the average fund earned an annualized average of 7.4 percent. The average fund investor earned just 5.9 percent.
- John C. Bogle, founder of the Vanguard funds, calculated that from 1984 through 2004, the 200 biggest U.S. stock funds gained an annual average of 9.9 percent—but the typical shareholder in those funds earned only 6.6 percent annually.
- In two studies I conducted in collaboration with researchers from the University of Indiana and the Ford Foundation, we found that in 1996, the typical shareholder at more than a dozen profitable U.S. stock funds actually lost money—and that, from 1998 through 2001, the average fund gained 5.7 percent annually while the typical fund investor gained only 1.0 percent. In one especially tragic case, Firsthand Technology Value Fund earned an average annual gain of 16 percent—but its typical investor *lost* 31.6 percent annually.
- Between 1973 and 2002, NASDAQ stocks gained an annual average of 9.6 percent. But because investors poured an astounding $1.1 trillion into

overpriced new stocks on NASDAQ between 1998 and 2000, just before the worst crash in a generation, the typical dollar invested on NASDAQ earned only 4.3 percent a year overall.

- From 1926 through 2002, investors in U.S. stocks earned an annual average of nearly 1.5 percentage points less than the stock market itself, thanks to their perennial habit of buying high and selling low.*

Earning as Much as What You Own

So how should you go about ensuring that your investments will not earn more than you do?

First, do not chase performance. Remember that the hot returns were probably earned by only a handful of people who either had the dumb luck to get in at the beginning or had a private route onto the inside track. Those who get in later—like you—will reach for hot returns and end up holding a fistful of cold ashes.

*Geoffrey C. Friesen and Travis R.A. Sapp, "Mutual Fund Flows and Investor Returns," *Journal of Banking & Finance* 31 (2007): 2796–2816; Oded Braverman, Shmuel Kandel, and Avi Wohl, "The (Bad?) Timing of Mutual Fund Investors," www.cepr.org/pubs/dps/DP5243.asp; John C. Bogle, "In Investing, You Get What You Don't Pay For," http://johncbogle.com/speeches/JCB_MS0205.pdf; Jason Zweig, "Funds That Really Make Money for Their Investors," *Money*, April 1997, 124–129; Jason Zweig, "What Fund Investors Really Need to Know," *Money*, June 2002, 110–115; Ilia Dichev, "What Are Stock Investors' Actual Historical Returns?," *American Economic Review* 97 (2007): 386–401.

Next, remember that big gains tend to come in very short sudden streaks. Often, stocks and funds earn their highest returns in a few days or weeks. Those spectacular gains remain in the long-term record, but they are a thing of the past. You would be foolish to count on more in the future.

What goes up must go down, and whatever went up the most tends to come down the hardest. Very high returns are likely to be followed by very low returns. If you missed the big gains, do you really want to grab onto the big losses that are likely to follow?

Many stocks and funds generate their greatest returns when they are small. Once those high returns attract the attention of millions of investors and the stock or fund grows larger, its best performance is probably already behind it.

The more volatile a stock or fund is—the more its price tends to bounce up and down—the more likely it is to catch your attention and tempt you to trade on the swings. Greater risk does *not* always mean greater return, precisely because big swings can lure you into buying and selling at just the wrong time. Resist the siren song of volatility and stick to slower, steadier stocks and funds that skip the short-term thrills for the certainty of long-term stability. And strap yourself in for the duration. If you don't need the money for years or decades, then you don't need to move it around every few weeks or months.

Safe Bets

- Match your holding periods to your horizons: If you are investing for retirement 30 years away, buy a total stock-market index fund and hold it continuously for the next three decades.

- Commit to a dollar-cost averaging or automatic investment plan that requires you to add a little bit of money every month.

- Embrace funds that charge short-term redemption fees, or penalties for frequent trading.

- Rebalance your holdings once a year.

- Track the performance of every investment you sell *after you sell it,* to learn whether you would have been better off holding on. The evidence suggests that trading will reduce your return by at least 1.5 percentage points per year—before tax and any trading costs! In investing, less is more.

Chapter Twenty-Two

How to Talk Back to Market Baloney

~

The Fine Art of Picking Apart Financial Propaganda

To keep your money safe, you must safeguard yourself not only from outright fraud, but from intellectual fakery—fast footwork in how the evidence is presented, slick marketing brochures that focus your attention on the wrong thing, statistical trickery that hides the truth in a blizzard of data.

The good news is that a few simple rules can enable you to screen out most of this kind of intellectual fakery. The bad news is that it is far more prevalent than outright fraud. It is everywhere—in newspapers and magazines, in advertisements, on television, and especially online. The Madoff scheme will go down in history for its size and boldness, but the cumulative toll of smaller scams is actually much greater in both the number of victims and the amount of money stolen from them. So you must stay vigilant and keep your skepticism as sharp as a razor.

Darrell Huff concluded his classic 1954 book *How to Lie with Statistics* (W. W. Norton) with a wonderful chapter entitled "How to Talk Back to a Statistic." He offered five questions you should always ask when confronted with a statistic that sounds convincing:

1. Who says so?
2. How does he know?
3. What's missing?
4. Did somebody change the subject?
5. Does it make sense?

In the same spirit, here are some guidelines on how to talk back to market baloney.

Take this claim from www.nystockreport.com that turned up as a banner ad on my Gmail account one day: "14,286% Penny Stock Gains: Our Penny Stock Picks are not only Free, But 100% Accurate."

Let's take Huff's questions in order.

Who Says So?

The names of the people behind NY Stock Report are nowhere to be found. The home page declares that "for almost a decade we have been alerting . . . " and "I want everyone to know . . . "and mentions an "Artificial Intelligence Computer Scientist." But clicking on the "About" page offers no explanation of who the "we" or the "I" might be, other than a mysterious reference to an "Editorial Director." (There's no further mention of the "Artificial Intelligence Computer Scientist.") A Google search on the name of the firm turned up only 14 hits on the entire Internet, none of them offering any more detail. The "Contact" page on the web site lists neither a phone number nor an address, although it does offer yet another blast of hype under the cloak of anonymity: "I can say with confidence that this is the most powerful money making opportunity in existence. If you sincerely want to accumulate vast wealth, then you must make this first step. . . . "

No one from NY Stock Report responded to my e-mailed requests for further information. Nor would anyone acknowledge my requests for comment.

How Does He Know?

A reputable and reliable investing approach spells out the evidence for a particular strategy and the sources of that evidence. For one good example, see "What Has Worked in Investing," at www.tweedy.com/resources/library_docs/papers/WhatHasWorkedInInvesting.pdf. Here, the partners at Tweedy, Browne Co. document their investing strategy by citing specific studies by finance professors and other academic researchers who have studied thousands of stocks over dozens of years and a variety of market conditions. In each case, they not only indicate what the evidence shows but how you can double-check their claims by going to the original sources.

In contrast, the NY Stock Report not only fails to tell you who "he" is, but offers no proof to back up its claims. There is simply no way you can validate the web site's assertions.

What's Missing?

In this case, what's missing is a sense of reality. Poke around on NY Stock Report and you will quickly see that the hot "returns" hyped by the web site are in penny stocks, the most illiquid and infrequently traded of all shares. Some of these stocks trade only a few hundred shares in an entire day; some, in fact, may not trade at all on some days.

One stock listed in the "Trades" section of the site (as of August 2009) was typical: "BANI," or Banneker, Inc., a microscopic Denver company that markets wristwatches and jewelry. (The firm is so small that it does not even file financial disclosure documents with the Securities and Exchange Commission.) NY Stock Report brags that you could have earned a 631 percent return if you had bought BANI stock at 1.08 cents per share on January 29, 2009, and sold it for 7.9 cents on February 9. (Note: This stock was last sighted trading below half a cent per share.)

Something else is missing: taxes.

If you hold on to a stock for one year or more and then sell it for a profit, the government will tax your gain at 0 percent to 15 percent, depending on your income. If you hold it for less than a year, the government will keep up to 35 percent of your profit. Therefore, you wouldn't have had a gain of more than 6.8 cents a share on BANI. Your gain (depending on your tax bracket) would have been as little as 4.4 cents per share after tax—*even if you could have done this trade for free.*

But, of course, you couldn't have. That's the next thing that's missing: the costs of trading.

The web site calculates BANI's return as if you had bought it for 1.08 cents per share and sold it for 7.9 cents per share. But most online brokerages charge around

$9.99 to trade a stock. You would have to buy roughly 1,000 shares of BANI just to cover the cost of buying them. (Putting up $1.08 for 100 shares and then paying $9.99 to execute the order wouldn't make much sense!)

It's a good general rule of thumb that your commission costs for trading a stock should be no higher than around 1 percent of the total value of the shares you are purchasing. To get your commission costs on trading BANI down to that level, you would need to buy 92,500 shares of this tiny stock. And if you entered such a massive buy order into so thin a market, you would drive the price sky-high.

So the web site can claim that BANI traded at 1.08 cents per share—but anybody who actually tried to buy a reasonable number of shares would have had to pay far more than 1.08 cents. And that, in turn, by raising the purchase price, would have vastly lowered the potential gain.

The same problem unfolds in reverse when you sell. Trying to sell 92,500 shares of an itty-bitty stock is like attempting to dump an ocean into a teacup. Any sensible buyer should—and will—ask what the seller might know that would prompt the unloading of so many shares. And that, in turn, would scare away just about any buyer, causing the price to fall far below the 7.9 cents quoted by the web site.

That's exactly what did happen to BANI. On February 11 and 12, 2009, the stock went from 6 cents a share to 3 cents on a massive wave of selling. If you had tried to unload your 92,500 shares into that selling panic, you would have driven the price even lower.

Thus, neither the 1.08 cents at the beginning nor the 7.9 cents at the end is a realistic price. A real live person trying to make real live trades could not have gotten in or out of this stock anywhere near those prices. You would probably have had to pay around 3 cents a share to buy— and would have been very lucky to get 3 cents when you got out.

In other words, that 631 percent gain is hypothetical, not real; no subscriber earned it, because none could have. Factor in the costs of brokerage and taxes, and it would take a near miracle just to break even on this trade.

In the real world, costs matter—and they matter a lot.

Did Somebody Change the Subject?

You bet.

The first time I heard about NY Stock Report, the return I could supposedly earn by following its tips was a scorching 14,286 percent. But the home page for its web site boasts about "over 2800% in stock gains from the past two years." Its "Services" page says its subscribers have earned "an average of 17% gains [per] month for the past 2 years." Its "About" section refers to "up to 650% gains." And its "Trades" page brags about an "Average of over 98% Increase." In fact, no matter where you click on this web site, you will get a different estimate for how high a mountain of money you could pile up by following its advice. (None of them are small, however.)

Another common technique (although it's unclear whether NY Stock Report does this) is to ignore the returns of strategies that failed—the problem of "survivorship bias" that we discussed in Chapters 7 and 12. There's a mysterious absence of money-losing trades on the NY Stock Report web site. You must always ask whether the portfolios presented actually reflect the returns of choices that were available at the time, or whether they were selected with 20/20 hindsight.

Does It Make Sense?

Ask yourself: If I knew how to earn 14,286 percent* on my money, would I tell anybody else how to do it? Or would I just keep it to myself until I became the richest person in the world?

---

*Or more than 2,800 percent, or up to 650 percent, or 17 percent per month, or over 98 percent, or whatever.

Next ask yourself: If I knew how to earn 14,286 percent and for some odd reason decided to tell other people how I do it, how much would I charge them to learn my secret? Would I boast to all comers that the service was "free" for the asking?

Those are the obvious questions; some subtler questions are worth asking, too.

NY Stock Report brags that its picks are "100% Accurate." In a highly uncertain world, how can any predictive activity ever be 100 percent accurate?

As we've already seen, even the annual average return of 7 percent on stocks, after inflation, may not be a sure thing. How could anyone possibly be able to earn up to 2,000 times more than that?

In fact, web sites like NY Stock Report are quite common, and there's nothing unusual about claims like these. Some of these sites are part of so-called pump-and-dump schemes, in which stock promoters mention a stock in e-mails that they blast out to thousands of subscribers. The promoters often buy the stock at depressed prices before they mention it. Then, when subscribers start to buy on the basis of the free advice, increasing demand for the shares and driving up the stock price, the promoters promptly dump it. The promoters can afford to make the advice free because they make so much money manipulating the stocks that they recommend to their subscribers.

There is no such thing as harmless hype. A site like NY Stock Report may seem too unsophisticated to fool a smart investor like you, but it's vital to remember that absolutely anyone can be hooked by crude appeals to greed. Thanks to the frailties of the human mind, a simple twist in circumstances can make suckers of us all. Remember what we learned about the bias blind spot in Chapter 17: If you think only *other people* can ever be suckers, that may lead you to drop your guard and end up a sucker yourself.

In investing, what separates the victims from the victors is discipline and skepticism. Ultimately, keeping your money safe is not very different from keeping your marriage sound: It requires hard work, devotion, attention to detail, and infinite patience. Spouses should live by their marriage vows; investors should abide by the Three Commandments. And you must take each day at a time, bearing in mind that surprises are the inevitable test of endurance.

Safe Bets

- From any claimed return, subtract a realistic estimate of expenses (at least two percentage points per year).
- Always ask the five basic questions.
- Always be sure you have followed the Three Commandments.

Acknowledgments

—— ∾ ——

EVEN A LITTLE BOOK is a big task.

This one is the product of all too many late nights, early mornings, and long weekends—all made possible by the indulgence of my family. With luck, my answer to everything will no longer be "I can't talk to you right now."

I would like to thank my agent, the peerless John Wright, for orchestrating this project. I am also very grateful to the extremely kind and wonderfully competent team at John Wiley & Sons (in alphabetical order): Tiffany Charbonier, Bill Falloon, Stacey Fischkelta, Emilie Herman, Pamela van Giessen, and Laura Walsh.

Finally, I thank my editors at the *Wall Street Journal*, Neal Templin and Ken Brown, for pretending not to notice that I was working on this book. Above all, I would like to thank my readers. Their criticisms have made me smarter, and their support has made me stronger. The intelligence, wisdom, and integrity of investors are a never-ending inspiration to me. I hope you will share your inspiration (and offer your criticism) at info@jasonzweig.com.